T4-AVD-188

STOP & THINK

10 Outstanding Advisors Provide

IMPORTANT FINANCIAL ADVICE
for YOU and YOUR FAMILY!

◆◆◆

Compiled and Edited by
Sydney LeBlanc • Lyn Fisher

Financial Forum Publishing

NOTICE: This publication is designed to provide accurate and authoritative information with regard to the subject matter covered. It is sold/distributed with the understanding the publisher and editors Lyn Fisher and Sydney LeBlanc are not engaged in rendering legal, accounting, investment or other professional services. Each chapter is expressly the opinion of that specific chapter's author.

LEGAL DISCLAIMER: The companies represented by the various chapters' authors featured in this book did not assist in the preparation of this report, and its accuracy and completeness are not guaranteed. The opinions of the authors are expressly their own, and not necessarily those of the individual firms or their affiliates. The material has been prepared, or is distributed, solely for informational purposes.

Copies of this book are available for purchase through:
Financial Forum Bookstore
http://www.ffbookstore.com
(tel) 435.750.0062
Discounts available for volume purchases.

ISBN: 978-0-9786010-4-1
Publisher:
Financial Forum Publishing & Communications
(tel) 435.787.2900

Printed in the United Sates of America

Thank you to the 10 advisors and their teams who made this book possible through their invaluable contributions.

A special thanks to Andrea Christensen, Mary Welsch, Alison Hobbs and Kimber Miller for their diligent work to help bring it to fruition.

And last but not least, thanks to John Crowther for the delightful cartoon he created for the cover that so effectively portrays the overall theme of the book.

TABLE OF CONTENTS

FOREWORD

How many times have you said to yourself, "If ONLY I had known earlier!" Or perhaps you have said to a friend, "WHY didn't you tell me this before?" We all have had experiences and have made decisions that we wish we could either erase or do over differently. In life, we all learn from our mistakes and so we try to take a positive approach and look at the good side of a bad experience.

But, when it comes to growing and preserving our hard-earned dollars and our life savings, it's important to be extremely careful about our decision-making processes. This is not the time for going on instinct or for doing-it-yourself. This is the major reason *STOP & THINK* was written by top wealth managers and financial advisors across the country. The book is a collaborative effort undertaken by those whom we consider to be among the most skilled and knowledgeable professionals in the financial services industry. All have extensive experience working with investors as they help them make educated decisions on important financial topics such as preparing for a medical crisis, coping with the death of a loved one, planning for retirement, investing and understanding the importance of charitable giving. You also will find a chapter especially written for small business owners that gives ideas on how to manage and preserve company wealth.

We have heard literally thousands of horror stories about investors losing their retirement money or their entire asset base because they either chose an inappropriate advisor or tried to manage their wealth alone. The last chapter in the book will help you identify the qualities of a trusted advisory firm. The advisors in this book tell their stories through first-hand accounts and case studies that help illustrate the need for professional advice and counsel.

STOP & THINK offers important advice that will hopefully leave a lasting impression on you, the reader, and encourage you to "stop and think" before making important financial decisions. These are the types of discussions the authors believe you should have with your wealth advisors, those who will help you realize your dreams and goals while still allowing you to sleep at night — worry free.

We hope you enjoy reading the book as much as we enjoyed producing it for you.

Sydney LeBlanc and Lyn Fisher

1. Clarity in Financial Goal Planning

Irwin L. Gross, RFC, CFS
Irwin Gross & Associates

Financial goal planning can be a formidable task. But it doesn't have to be and, moreover, it can be enjoyable and bring you a sense of financial confidence. The purpose of this chapter is to explain why it is important to plan before you invest. How to reach your financial goals is based on setting a financial goal and sticking with your financial goal planning. I'll show you how to organize your financial goals into manageable steps through a financial goal-planning process. So let's get started.

Why Plan?

So you're trying to determine what financial product you need, what estate documents to draft and what insurance to purchase. Wouldn't it be easier to make that determination if you had an idea of *what* you wanted to do and *why* you wanted to do it before you went into the purchase mode?

Let's discuss three hypothetical situations:

1. Dan and Alice asked their attorney to draft a will (product). The attorney provided the documents as requested, but failed to consider the following:

STOP & THINK

- Could they have afforded to give money away to reduce estate taxes?
- Which was more important to them, estate settlement costs or asset distribution and retention strategies?
- Did they want to protect these assets from creditors, debtors, divorce and taxes for themselves, their children and possibly other generations?

Would Dan and Alice have thought to ask these questions? Probably not.

2. Sam and Felicia had some cash to invest. They went to a stockbroker to receive investing advice. Of the many options available, the broker provided some good-performing stocks and other specific investment products. They did get advice on investing the money, but some items were not considered. Here are a few examples:

- What overall tax effect would this have and should that have been considered?

- How should this money be titled for asset protection needs and estate planning purposes?

- How would this investment coordinate with their entire portfolio, including their 401(k), to allow them proper diversification?

3. Nathan had a friend who passed away suddenly. Nathan then decided to call an insurance agent to purchase a term life insurance policy (product) and was asked how much he wanted to buy. The agent then procured the policy and the policy was issued. Here are some questions that should have been considered:

- How much insurance did Nathan really need to cover his family?

- How long did he need this coverage? Accordingly, what type of policies should have been purchased?

- What risk was he willing to take that could be assumed by him or passed to the insurance company?

- How should this policy have been owned? If it was owned improperly, it could have subjected the proceeds to estate tax, income tax or have exposed the policy to creditors.

All three of these examples give you an idea of how one independent decision can affect other decisions you make and that is the whole point.

This is the purpose of considering a comprehensive, coordinated financial plan that is more holistic than product-oriented; one that is centered on you and your wealth advisor determining your mission, vision, values and goals. It is extremely important that you obtain clarity on what you want to do and why you want to do it before you ever go below your planning horizon and start to look at solutions. (See Clarity Horizon Chart below.)

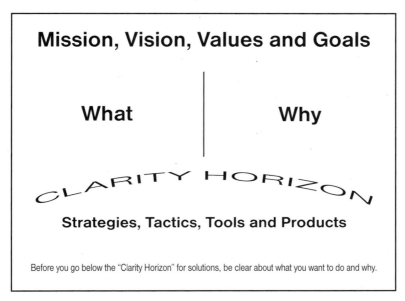

Mission, Vision, Values and Goals

What | **Why**

CLARITY HORIZON

Strategies, Tactics, Tools and Products

Before you go below the "Clarity Horizon" for solutions, be clear about what you want to do and why.

Solutions become much easier once you become clear on *what* you want to do and *why* you want to do it. This type of planning coordinates your insurance, legal issues, taxes and investments all at one time. This can take significant time, but it is important for you to work with your wealth advisor on this to gain the clarity you both need. The next section will show you how.

How to Gain Clarity Before Solutions

The first issue is to find a wealth advisor who believes in objectively providing goal-oriented planning, not product-based planning. To maintain objectivity, I believe a fee-based approach is best because there may be a hidden agenda or a conflict of interest with some production-driven solutions.

On the next page you'll find a list of sample questions to assist you in selecting the right wealth advisor for you.

List of Planner's Unique Abilities

Do your advisors possess or have access to the following abilities?

1. Understand and interpret your goals, dreams and desires reducing then to a written statement that will guide the planning process?

2. Assemble, organize and manage unique abilities in order to accomplish strategic planning objectives?

3. Work with your tax professional to uncover and diagnose complex tax problems?

4. Design a financial model that accurately reflects how your plan will function today, over time and at life expectancy?

5. Initiate creative planning ideas that accomplish specific planning objectives?

6. Have access to a team of experts for advanced planning strategies?

7. Design insurance and investment strategies that accomplish planning objectives to your maximum advantage?

8. Have access to a team of experts for advanced insurance strategies?

9. Interpret and translate complex income tax legislation into understandable opportunities?

10. Design charitable planning strategies that focus taxable assets toward self-directed social capital?

11. Work with drafters of state-of-the-art legal documents?

PHASE I — Gaining Clarity

Step 1: Think About Your Future. Let's start with a question: If we were sitting here three years from today looking back on those three years, what would you want to have happened that would have made you happy about your progress and success, both personally and professionally?

It sounds like a simple question, but if you study the various words, each one is important. Initially we talk of taking you three years into the future to eliminate what we call the tyranny of the urgent[1] By removing today's issues and stresses, we're in a position of actually looking at what you want — not what we need to do today to solve your immediate issues.

What is an example of a planning answer versus a product answer?

Someone asked me what it would take if a client gave me $1 million of capital for investments in their portfolio. My response was not what they expected because I did not immediately jump to sell a product or provide an easy solution. I began to ask some questions:

- What is this money going to accomplish for you and when?
- What is your tax position?
- How will this money be invested to coordinate with other investments?
- Is this money for current needs or a future need?
- What is your tax perspective and investment risk perspective?
- How should this investment be titled?
- Is this money for your use or possibly for someone else?

The answers to these questions have an effect from an estate planning, tax and asset protection perspective.

Obviously, as you look at an investment portfolio, you should take into consideration all of the investments to create the investment policy statement — even if your investment advisor representative is only to manage a portion of that portfolio.

Why am I suggesting this? As each investment is looked at, one question should be, is it in tax-advantaged vehicles, such as qualified plans, or is it in the open portfolio? This has a bearing from the tax perspective. As you look at the entire portfolio, you're also trying to make sure that the overlap of the different models are viewed, not independently of each other, but as an entire portfolio. Balance is also needed as to your risk tolerance. Risk tolerance is your ability to feel okay with losses in your portfolio or market volatility. Risk tolerance is important for you to know, to understand how much risk

---

1 Originally documented by Charles Hummel in his 1967 essay and 1999 inspirational book, "Tyranny of the Urgent."

you are willing to take to achieve an investment goal. The higher your risk tolerance, the more risk you are willing to take.

Simply stated, risk tolerance addresses, 1) conservation of capital, 2) growth of capital and 3) current income needs.

As you can see, the answers to the question of "what should I do with this $1 million?" should never be looked at in a vacuum, and all actions should be coordinated with the entire plan.

I do believe you are beginning to see the difference between a planning approach and a product approach. Many times, the fee-based advisor oversees the product professionals and as such is strictly on the side of their clients. This works because clients are at a disadvantage. They are trying to coordinate the planning activity alone because, "We do not know what we don't know."

Now that you are beginning to understand what a comprehensive plan is and why it is important, let's take the next step.

Step 2: Your Goals and How You Can Accomplish Them. Now that we've taken you into the future, you're able to look back and project what it is you want to do and how you're going to get there. Now, all of this is centered on your goals, your mission, your vision and your values. If your wealth advisor asks the right questions, it will help empower you. You can't let the questions stop after the initial question of "what is your goal?" You will probably give a fairly general answer. But then you must go into the second phase of this goal-oriented question. For example, there are three major issues that need to be addressed:

1. What is stopping you from reaching your goals — the dangers, the thoughts that keep you up at night?

2. What are the opportunities that you want to move forward on that will assist you in obtaining these goals? These are the thoughts that keep you excited. These are the things you really want to do.

3. What are the strengths that you bring to the table that allow you to enhance the opportunities and maximize your strengths so you continue to move forward?

This is all part of goal planning. Goal planning is like taking a rope and pulling the rope forward where you want it to go. Obviously, if you try to push that rope, the bends and the twists make it much more difficult. Just remember that is part of the challenge; so try not to get discouraged. Just keep at it.

Now that you are beginning to gain clarity of what you want to do and why, we can begin to focus on the three major components of the Planning Hierarchy. They are: Financial Independence, Family, and Social Capital. Each will have a bearing on the other. (See Planning Hierarchy Chart below.)

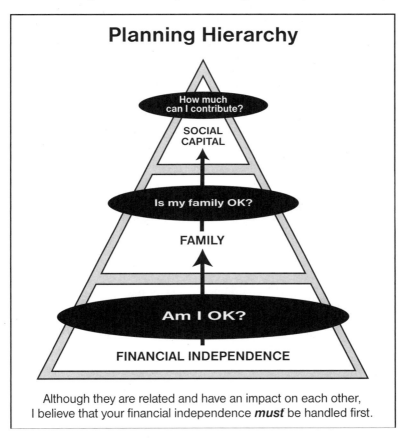

Planning Hierarchy

How much can I contribute?

SOCIAL CAPITAL

Is my family OK?

FAMILY

Am I OK?

FINANCIAL INDEPENDENCE

Although they are related and have an impact on each other, I believe that your financial independence **must** be handled first.

PHASE II — Determine Goals

The Planning Hierarchy: Three Main Components Explained

The overall planning perspective starts with the planning hierarchy. The planning hierarchy, which is the triangle, always starts with financial independence as the base of the planning hierarchy. The next step up will be what you want to do for your family, and the next and last step in this hierarchy is social capital.

Let me define each one of these components:

Step 1: Gain Financial Independence. This is the ability to do what you want to do when you want to do it. It is understanding how much is enough. It is the first phase of determining what makes you happy and what makes you dissatisfied.

Cash flow is important to your sense of well-being and confidence. Look at your current financial position first to determine your financial independence. To look at your current position, you need to determine current cash flow. It is very difficult to understand where you want to be unless you understand where you are today. The current cash flow model is one of the most difficult things for a client to truly undertake. Most people do not live on budgets. It may take some time to have a complete understanding of what your current position looks like.

If you're in business, you have to take a look at what the business will and won't pay for when you are considering financial independence, because the business may or may not be around indefinitely. Obviously, you can initially work with close guesses, but the more accurate it is, the more accurate the projections.

The next step to determining financial independence is to ask the following: What do you want to do? What kind of lifestyle do you want?

Again, this goes back to goal planning. Money is not the goal. Instead, it is what money can do for you. Now that you have more time than you did before you retired, does financial independence mean more travel? More time with the grandchildren? More time spent in the community and activities surrounding it, be they political or charitable? These are just some of the areas that need definitions when you determine what financial independence means to you.

A client once said to me, "When I retire, I simply want to maintain the lifestyle I have now." That started out at $75,000 a year in today's environment. Then he added, "Since I have time I would want a second home in North Carolina — on a lake." We added money for that to his goal planning list, and then he said, "With a dock for the lake boat." He then said, "I now have grandchildren so it needs to be at least a three-bedroom house, and I want to pay for a family vacation for my two children and their families each year." By the time we were finished with his true goal, we were up to

$130,000 per year.

Step 2: Define Family Priorities. The definition of family and what you want to accomplish with family becomes the second item to consider as you move up the planning hierarchy triangle. Sometimes family can be not just your own children, but it can also extend to parents, nieces, nephews, grandchildren, great-grandchildren and others.

A lot of this comes to the forefront as you talk about family values and how you want to pass these values on to them, and especially when issues of estate planning objectives come up in discussions with your wealth advisor. These types of conversations are not feasible until financial independence becomes very clear to you. Here is when you realize you are in the position to do what you want, when you want, and how you want to do it.

Also, do not forget family milestones in planning, because they may have an effect on financial independence. Some of these milestones include: college funding for children or grandchildren; assistance for relatives including elderly parents; divorce; death; weddings; births and other events.

Step 3: *Build Social Capital.* The last item on the planning hierarchy triangle is defined as those funds that will not pass through your family, or funds that you will not depend on for your personal financial independence. To have these types of funds you must be relatively affluent, but based on your financial picture your net worth could be as low as $2 million.

All of it goes back to the question, What do you want to do and why? Don't question if the goal is attainable yet — just dream. It is up to the planner or wealth advisor and you to determine what it will take to get there. A good wealth advisor not only provides creative solutions, but also acts as a catalyst to help in getting things done.

> What do you want to do and why? Don't question if the goal is attainable yet — just dream. It is up to the planner or wealth advisor and you to determine what it will take to get there.

Estate Tax and Involuntary Social Capital

If your estate is worth $1 million (or possibly a higher amount), it is your choice whether to pay in the form of taxes or in tax deductible contributions. You can make a donation to your favorite charity or pay the tax dollars. This choice of either contribution or taxes is known as social capital. In other words, without the proper planning, these types of estates will have social capital (estate taxes or administrative settlement costs) paid out in either settlement costs or estate taxation. Estate taxation is a form of involuntary social capital. Many clients want to be in control of their social capital. They believe they can have more funds put to better use without the bureaucratic snags and governmental intervention. They also may feel close to specific charitable causes.

How much of the estate taxes paid goes to social causes? It is less than 35% with the balance going to other governmental issues. (See Chart below.)

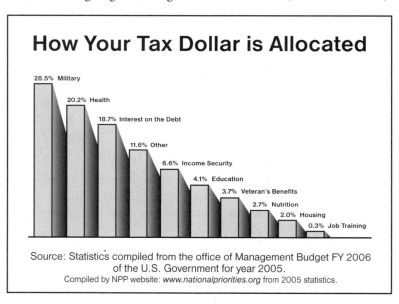

How Your Tax Dollar is Allocated

28.5% Military

20.2% Health

18.7% Interest on the Debt

11.6% Other

6.6% Income Security

4.1% Education

3.7% Veteran's Benefits

2.7% Nutrition

2.0% Housing

0.3% Job Training

Source: Statistics compiled from the office of Management Budget FY 2006 of the U.S. Government for year 2005.
Compiled by NPP website: *www.nationalpriorities.org* from 2005 statistics.

What are Your True Values?

Now that you've come this far, what is next? You can begin to move forward and question some of the values that center on each of these objectives.

By looking at your values statement, you're now in the position of making all plans revolve around what is most important to you. One of the questions to consider is, What is the most important thing to you about money? You start to think about how to make your life become more significant. Are the material things the most important items? Wht is significant to you is very intrinsic. You can't put a price on it. It is something that you feel. Nobody can question that feeling.

Again, this question appears to be very simple on the surface, but it becomes extremely complex as you begin to dig deeper into it. The first few things that come to mind when people think about financial security are, can they send their children to college? Will they have enough money? Your wealth advisor should be asking you these questions. Once the obvious answers are given, your wealth advisor will dig even deeper. He or she will ask you to think about the following: Suppose you have enough money for your financial independence, your kids have gone through college and you've provided for your family. Are you ready to create a family mission statement to pass on to future generations? Every family's mission statement is different. It would have different beliefs and different goals, but the idea is to give your family an identity and a long-range goal that fits into the overall plan.

PHASE III

Step 1: Priority Phase. Decide what to do first and prioritize your action plan. As you answer these questions, you now go into the third phase in which you develop a list of priorities. What is important, urgent, and tactical? If you find that things are not clear, you need to gain more clarity on that particular item before you can start to move forward on it. If you find that it is strategic instead of tactical, more discussion needs to take place as far as trying to determine what needs to happen to accomplish a particular item. In other words, break down big issues into smaller parts so they become easier to handle. Obviously, if an issue is not as important as something else, then it won't take the same level of priority in your planning.

Eat the elephant — one bite at a time. Determining what is important, clear, tactical and urgent becomes first priority. From there you decide what the next steps are to accomplish your goals. You begin to lay out the plan for the next year — quarter by quarter. We all have busy schedules, but it becomes very important to prioritize your action plan. So, as the African proverb goes, you have to "eat an elephant one bite at a time." By prioritizing each step, you can move forward and continue to accomplish your goals one bite at a time, rather than feel overwhelmed.

Step 2: The Discovery Phase. Obtain clarity of vision. Go back to Phase I and revisit the Discovery Process. This process starts when you begin to dream and think about what you want to do in the future. The particular technique that I have found most effective is to use a questionnaire. If you are married, the process is for you and your spouse to complete these questionnaires separately without discussing them with each other. The advantage of completing a questionnaire in this fashion is that there is no implied pressure from either party on the other in answering the questions of what they truly would want to have happen in the three areas of the Planning Hierarchy (Financial Independence, Family, and Social Capital).

How Are You "Wired?"

I have found it extremely advantageous to have a client consider personality profiling and use a specific method of this profiling. It indicates how a client is "wired," meaning whether they are heavy into fact-finding, quick to make decisions, if they want to get their hands dirty and do all the work, and if they are reliable at following through and getting all of this information.

This type of analysis gives us an indication of who they are, which helps us in working with them. There is a tremendous value for the husband and wife who come to understand their differences.

Step 3: Strategy Risk Profile and Complexity Risk Profile. Strategy risk tolerance is a completely different level of understanding than what we have on investment risk tolerance. Strategy risk tolerance addresses the individual's ability to get involved with complex issues, lose privacy, suffer public embarrassment, go through civil litigation and other difficult circumstances. Couple this with the complexity risk profile which involves dealing with multiple advisors, lengthy meetings, abstract discussions, irrevocable decisions and other complex issues, and you now have a better understanding of the client's likes, dislikes and threshold for planning "pain." This helps separate what may be a great idea but may not fit the client's threshold for complexity risk profiles. It may be a good idea, but perhaps not for a particular client.

Now that you have decided what and why, prioritized the list and profiled characteristics and risk, what is next?

PHASE IV

Your Advisory Team: An Honest Evaluation

Let's discuss the team of advisors you currently have in place as defined in the chart on page 14 and determine the value each team member has to you. A team consists of various advisors needed to accomplish a project, perhaps an attorney, CPA, insurance agent, investment advisor representative, your wealth advisor, or others. Some may serve dual roles, which you can determine by weighing their knowledge, reliability, relationship ability and self-orientation (their trustworthiness).

Consider the following:

- How often do you speak with them?
- How comfortable are you that they are looking out for your interests first?
- When they suggest solutions do you agree they should implement them?
- Do they follow through on implementing the solutions?
- How effective are they at managing the implementation?
- Are they proactively suggesting additional solutions to implement?

These are some of the pointed questions to address when determining each advisor's importance and value to the team. Not only do you want the best team possible, but you also want those who can assist you in this comprehensive planning process.

This is where the team manager or objective fee-based wealth advisor can help. They become your advocate. As you can see on the Tapestry of Wealth™ Chart (next page), this person is in exactly the same position you are. They can help with the "I do not know what I don't know" issue.

Now let's take a look at investments, not from a perspective of which investment fund/manager you use, but rather the services you want your team of advocates to provide.

Investment Advisory Services

What do you want your investment advisor representative to do for you? The fee that you pay for investment management services may have a bearing on services you want from your investment advisor representative, so again, be clear. Are you receiving these services now? Some of these services you may want to experience so you can decide if they are important or not.

Here are some management services to consider:

- Evaluation of your objectives
- Objective performance evaluation
- Consolidated reporting/tracking
- Asset allocation design
- Independent monthly auditing

STOP & THINK

- Independent quarterly reviews
- Tax planning of gains and losses
- Income/cash flow flexibility
- Money manager research
- Multiple investment and managerial options
- Comprehensive fee structure

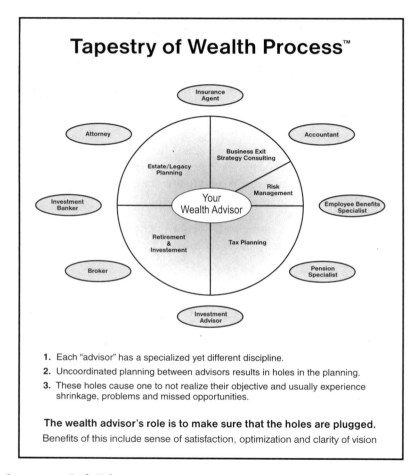

Tapestry of Wealth Process™

1. Each "advisor" has a specialized yet different discipline.
2. Uncoordinated planning between advisors results in holes in the planning.
3. These holes cause one to not realize their objective and usually experience shrinkage, problems and missed opportunities.

The wealth advisor's role is to make sure that the holes are plugged.

Benefits of this include sense of satisfaction, optimization and clarity of vision

Investment Risk Tolerance

Most firms require clients to complete an initial investment risk tolerance questionnaire. I believe that this investment risk tolerance should be done annually. As changes occur in a client's life, so does their ability to feel comfortable with the risk of losing principal.

There are numerous ways to apply this risk tolerance test in creating a "written investment policy statement" for a client. Do you have a written investment policy statement? This document is tailored to your goals, risk, objectives and needs. It is your clear investment roadmap. Either your investment advisor representative can implement this for you, or a third-party money manager he or she has hired will do it for you while your wealth advisor oversees it.

In many cases, clients look to their financial planner as their "wealth coach" and advocate. Think of a sports team; the coach is the one responsible for holding all team members accountable, seeing shortfalls in members, reassigning players to correct positions and making sure as things change, they react . They do not do it alone. Players and assistant coaches all support the team.

Now that you have worked with your "coach" and defined:

- What you want to do
- Why you want to do it
- Found out the dangers, opportunities, strengths
- Prioritized those that are urgent, tactical and important
- Profiled characteristics
- Defined unique abilities
- Rated the advisory team

What is next?

PHASE V

Step 1: The Analytical Process — Audits. This truly gets into the details and auditing of all the information you need to help you make wise choices. It is highly analytical, involving various technology programs, and includes details of all you own and have in place. This is the process that will provide you with the tools to make smart decisions. It weighs the pros and cons of all aspects and looks at your current position. This is where the gaps and opportunities are explored. I have chosen to trademark this specific process that I use for my clients as the Tapestry of Wealth Process™ because it weaves all aspects of your life together to make the fabric of your life into the picture you want.

Step 2: The Financial Check-Up and the Comprehensive Technology Review — Options. These steps verify exactly where you are now, financially. An audit of investment statements, brokerage accounts and banks, real estate holdings and all other assets is performed. What do you really own, how much are you worth today and how diversified are you? Titling is important for estate income tax and with asset protection purposes. Contingency planning — some of the dangers are considered as well as how you have protected against them. What insurance do you have in force including life, disability, long term care, liability and others? Are they all performing the way they were "sold"? Are the deductibles correct? Are the amounts of coverage appropriate for current needs?

What are the different aspects of your plan to consider?

- Cash flow — income and expenses
- Financials including net worth and assets by ownership
- Financial independence projections for today and the future
- Income taxes currently and also viewed at financial independence
- Estate taxes and estate settlement costs
- Survivor planning
- Contingency planning, including liability and health issues such as long term care
- Education planning for children or others
- Investment modeling and investment policy statement
- Investment analysis of existing holdings compared to goals and analysis
- Social capital planning
- Coordination with business issues if you are a business owner

As the analysis is completed and options are discussed, the next phase of the detailed analysis process begins. This is where the various advisors come together in a coordinated fashion, all orchestrated by the "coach." This allows you to make sure all your advisors are on the same page. These advisors and planners are hired to try to bolster your financial position. From this discussion and analysis among advisors, agreements are reached and the next phase occurs.

Step 3: The Comparative Technique and Financial Freedom — Solutions. Again, you are involved in the process as the advisors have all agreed on various solutions based on the analysis. The plan, your goals, testing the discovery phase on risk, complexity and values are all considered. You are ready to make decisions to move forward, postpone actions or scrap some altogether. The difference is you now have all the information needed to make a wise choice, and your advisors have considered the pros and cons of each before ever reaching this point.

What is next?

PHASE VI

Implementation through the Action Plan Developed

As you now understand, implementation could not occur until you had clarity on what and why. Everything was centered on those two elements in the analysis phase. Product was the last item to consider after solutions were agreed on so you could move toward your goals. Only then should your advisor research the market to find the product that fits the solution for your unique needs.

What is the proper level of support at implementation? Implementation goes far beyond simply making sure the product is put into place. Implementation is ensuring that all team members are working toward getting the job done. This could be as simple as implementing a trust, limited partnership or an insurance contract.

One of my clients thought that his life insurance policy, which named his wife as beneficiary, was a simple task and that it had been taken care of. His estate was more than $3 million and the life insurance policy added another $2 million, so the estate tax would have been approximately $500,000 of the death benefit, as it would be included in the estate.

Current tax law indicates an existing life insurance policy would be included in your estate for estate tax purposes. In order for this contract to pass outside of the estate, numerous things need to happen: You need to avoid transferring the contract and falling into an income tax trap. You want to avoid the three-year rule of putting this back into your estate and avoid gift tax issues and potential income tax issues. If done incorrectly, you will fall into the tax traps.

In addition, as you set up these various vehicles, there might be other legal requirements that need to take place, such as in an Irrevocable Life Insurance Trust where an annual Crummey Letter (named after an individual who challenged the IRS and won the right to apply his annual insurance premiums toward his gift tax exclusion) must be sent out to maintain this as exclusion for estate tax purposes. Discuss this letter with your wealth advisor.

As this points out, implementation is not simply placing a product, tactic or solution. It's making sure it is placed properly and all the details are taken care of. Who is assisting you in getting this accomplished? I believe that is part of the wealth advisor's role.

The Care and Treatment of Business Owners

Many of our clients are business owners. As a business owner, there is a significant amount of assets that are tied up in illiquid entities. If there is more than one partner in that business, business agreements should play an important role in your personal planning. If there are no partners in the business, then a decision has to be made: What are the future plans for that business and at what point will they be made and implemented? This type of coordination between business activity and personal activity is often overlooked.

Concerning the buy/sell agreement, consideration should be given as to whether it is a corporate document or a cross-purchase document. Obviously, this will have a significant difference on tax perspectives depending upon how the document(s) are structured.

A Reality Check

Are business insurance policies taken into consideration in the planning for liquidity or survivor needs?

If you are a business owner and getting close to retirement, what type of exit strategy has been put in place?

If there are documents such as a buy/sell agreement, what are the terms and conditions in the event of a disability?

Has this been dealt with in employment contracts to make sure that the proper tax issues have not been overlooked?

You and your wealth advisor should also look at various corporate strategies that could save taxes, such as medical reimbursement plans, properly structured health programs, and a review of the qualified plans that may make a difference. Qualified plans should be reviewed as to who you want to provide the most benefits for. Additionally, items that may be deductible through the business may not be deducted personally. This should be a discussion with your CPA. As you can see, these issues (and more) can be very complicated and should be examined carefully by experienced professionals like your team, your CPA and your attorney.

The Value-Added Experience

You now feel you have it all done and you can forget about it. Maybe not. Things change!

As we continue to move through the process of Clarity, Prioritization, Audits, Options, Solutions and Implementation, how do you know if you are on track? This is where most transactional — or product-oriented — plans fall short, in my opinion. Once the product — trust, insurance, or investment — is in place, planning ceases. It should continue to provide the sense of financial well-being. This is why annual monitoring of the plan, the goals and the investments is a valued option.

Why is this important? Life has a way of changing. This monitoring also keeps you on track and makes your wealth advisor or team accountable to see the items through that they have agreed to get done. It may take several years to finalize a plan and then changes occur in the family, economy or business which is to be expected and integrated into the plan. So how can your wealth advisor react to that without the proper monitoring?

Many of our clients call us their babysitter; others refer to us as their motivator; still others refer to us as their sleep insurance. Whatever they call us, it boils down to ongoing support and monitoring to keep everything on track. How many of you religiously follow the exercise routine the trainer lays out for you — when the trainer is not there?

This ongoing experience allows you to constantly verify where you are compared to where you want to be. It also allows you to buy your time back, be in control, and eliminate some of the "you do not know what you don't know" issues. That is value.

Last But Not Least, Keys to Planning

Following I have listed some keys to planning that are crucial to the success of your plan and achieving your goals. One of the most important keys is,

If you do not plan first — how will you know if it fits?

STOP & THINK

Let's review the highlights:

- Define what you want to do and the way to do it before any solution is considered.
- Find an objective, fee-based wealth advisor who puts you first—not product.
- Dream — what makes something important to you?
- Take yourself into the future so you *can* dream.
- Look at the pros and cons so wise decisions can be made.
- Prioritize and eliminate the overwhelming.
- Have someone oversee implementation when a solution is agreed on.
- Buy back your time and hire knowledgeable people.
- Stay on track.
- Monitor the results.
- Stay on top of life as it changes.

Irwin Gross
Irwin Gross & Associates
800 Fairway Drive, Suite 370
Deerfield Beach, FL 33441-1831
954.429.0090 or 800.334.5172 (tel)
Irwin.Gross@LFG.com

Irwin L. Gross is a Private Wealth Advisor in South Florida. He has helped affluent clients coordinate their financial world, saving them time and creating a plan for their future for more than 34 years.

Irwin graduated from the University of Miami in 1971 with a Finance Degree. Over the years, Irwin Gross & Associates has grown to be one of the premier fee-based Financial Planning and Wealth Coaching firms. Through a trademarked process, Irwin created and developed the Tapestry of Wealth Process™, a customized "Plan", to meet the objectives of his client's long-term goals. He is one of fewer than 250 people trained in a Discovery and Clarity process called Legacy Planning™; and only one of 100 people in the country trained to be an Ambassador for the Ultimate Gift Experience™. The Ultimate Gift process requires mutigenerational planning.

Irwin serves on two Boards: The Hurricane Club, and a national organization, The Resource Group. He chairs the Financial Planning Committee for The Resource Group and belongs to various industry organizations, including The Palm Beach Estate Planning Council and the International Association of Advisors in Philanthropy. Irwin has also been published in various local and national publications in the financial industry.

Eileen, his wife of 32 years, and he live in Weston Hills, Florida where they are members of Weston Hills Country Club as he is an avid golfer. He is also on the Board of the Men's Club at Weston Hills Country Club.

2. Investing 101: The Myths, the Facts, and All that Lies Between

Michael Booker, CFP®, ChFC, CFS, BCAA
Financial Synergies Asset Management, Inc.

When I first entered the financial services field in the early 1980s, I was told there were irrefutable investment facts that I needed to be aware of to be a successful advisor. I wanted to be the best financial advisor I could be, so I dutifully learned all of them. But, there was a problem — after a few years I discovered that most of these truths were really myths. As I sit here writing this chapter, I am still somewhat astonished that virtually all of these "truths" are still alive and well here in the 21st century — even though investors have lost fortunes abiding by them!

My goal is to separate what is truth from what is myth. You may find that *your truth* is *my myth* simply because they have been mainstays in our investment culture for so long. They are the ultimate survivors. English novelist Virginia Woolf was right when she said, "*It is much harder to kill a myth than a reality.*" With all due respect to Ms. Woolf, I am going to kill these myths with facts, because it has also been said:

"The truth shall set you free."

STOP & THINK

- MYTH #1: *Markets Are Predictable.*

> "There are two types of investors – those who
> don't know where the market is headed and those
> who don't know they don't know."
> — Anonymous

The thought here is that markets can be predicted by using technical analysis, a method of evaluating securities by relying on the assumption that charting market data, such as price, volume, and open interest, can help predict future (usually short-term) market trends. This is extraordinary because using this axiom, one can be fully invested in the market to benefit as it rises and totally out of the market before it drops.

- FACT #1: *Markets Are Anything BUT Predictable.*

Predicting the market is a concept that has been proliferated almost exclusively by the professional investment community as an effective marketing tool to prospective clients. In fact, William Bernstein, famous portfolio theorist, says there is actually a third type of investor to be added to the above quote: *"The investment professional who knows he or she doesn't know, but whose livelihood depends on appearing to know."*

The one-sided pile of evidence is overwhelming and convincingly demonstrates that markets are not predictable. I will quote some famous studies on the subject and we can move on. David Dreman, noted author, contrarian-style money manager and analyst, conducted an academic study that meticulously tracked the "expert's" opinions dating back to 1929 and found that these gurus were beat by the market an astonishing 77% of the time! In many similar studies, underperformance is a recurring theme with the average rate of underperformance a remarkable 75%.

Just for the sake of argument, let's assume someone actually had the ability to predict markets. No matter what this magical method would be, it would have an extremely short shelf life. Why? Because once this method became publicly known, it would cease to be effective because everyone would start employing it. For example, in 1991 a money manager named Michael O'Higgins published a book and system titled *Beating the Dow*. His "Dogs of the Dow" concept entailed buying the 10 most out-of-favor stocks in the Dow Jones 30 and keeping them until they eventually reversed direction. This contrarian technique worked well as out of favor stocks did tend to recover and regain investors' favor.

By the mid 1990s, more than 20 billion of investment fund dollars were placed in Dogs of the Dow investment vehicles marketed by Wall Street. Predictably, the Dogs of the Dow soon began to consistently underperform the overall market during the last half of the '90s. Michael O'Higgins stated, "The strategy became too popular." Like all investment fads, it eventually failed due to its success. Once everyone began to buy the Dogs of the Dow, they ceased being dogs! His unique method became mainstream.

- **MYTH #2:** *Market Timing Works Because Markets are Predictable.*

> *"How could I have been so mistaken as to have trusted the experts?"*
> – John F. Kennedy after the Bay of Pigs debacle

Here's the idea: Because technical analysis allows one to predict the future course of the market, one should be fully invested in the market when it is about to go up and should be out of the market right before it is about to go down. I can't argue with that — all gain and no pain. Sign me up!

- **FACT #2:** *Market Timing DOES NOT Work.*

Market timing is the granddaddy of all investment myths. Though I will present some academic studies that show this technique to be completely unsound and deeply flawed, it survives in our current investment landscape as a major player. Twenty-five years ago, I would never have dreamed that I would be writing a chapter about investment myths where market timers were still worthy of serious discussion. Let's get to the facts.

A study published in the February 2001 issue of *Financial Analyst Journal* is very instructive. The authors analyzed a variety of monthly, quarterly, and annual timing strategies from 1929 through 1999 and compared the results against a buy-and-hold strategy for the same time periods. As you might expect, there were more than a million different outcomes. The buy-and-hold strategy outperformed the market timing strategy 99.8% of the time.

Too long a time frame? Not valid in this modern super-computer era? A well-regarded study by Richard Woodward and Jess Chua, professors at the University of Calgary, focused on a more recent time frame of the last 54 years. Over this period, they cite that the market advanced in 36 years, broke even in three years and declined in just 15. Thus, the odds are almost three to one against investors when their money is in cash instead of stocks.

The professors concluded that investing in the market long-term works better than market timing because the gains from being in stocks far outweigh the losses incurred in bear markets. For market timing to actually outperform the buy-and-hold strategy, the market timer must call the market direction, in a very precise manner, 70% of the time. No one has ever accomplished this over a meaningful time frame.

A piece entitled "Likely Gains from Market Timing," by Nobel Laureate William F. Sharpe, for whom the Sharpe Ratio is named, states, "Barring any devastating market declines similar to those of The Great Depression, it seems likely that gains of little more than 4% per year from timing should be expected from a manager whose forecasts are *truly prophetic*."

Sharpe further determined that a manager who attempts to time the market must be right roughly three times out of four, merely to match the overall performance of those competitors who don't. There are two reasons for this. First, such managers will frequently have a percent of funds in cash or cash equivalents when the market is going up, thus losing the opportunity of full participation in the rising market. Second, they will incur transaction costs when switches are made, further dragging down performance.

Yet another study by Professor H. Negat Seybun, of the University of Michigan, found that 95% of significant market gains over the 30-year period from the mid-1960s through the mid-1990s came on just 90 of 7,500 trading days. If you happened to miss those 90 days, just over 1% of the total, the spectacular gains investors experienced over the period would have been *nonexistent*.

The practices of mutual fund managers who employ market timing have been great indicators as to what *not* to do. An analysis of their cash position is a great example of this. For example, a very high cash position would indicate caution on the part of the fund manager and coincides almost perfectly with the low points in the market in 1970, 1974, 1982, the end of 1987, late 1990, 1994, and 2002. These periods represented a perfect opportunity for market timers to have been fully invested to capture a market poised to go straight up. Yet their cash positions were at all-time highs, so they missed out on the impending market ascent.

On the other hand, market timing mutual funds had cash balances near all-time lows in March of 2000 — just before the market began its now-infamous decline. The experts were perfectly, and so painfully, wrong again!

To be sure, the only "confirmation" I have ever seen showing market timing as an effective strategy are those "studies" conducted by the market timers themselves. The fact that investors and professional money managers still employ market timing at all is a testament to the power this concept has as a marketing tool, since it taps so deeply into our fear and loathing of participating in the market when it is going south.

You may have already figured out that I am not a big fan of the experts, especially the ones that claim to predict the future. I absolutely believe in the importance of competence and expertise in all vocations, but when someone tells me what the market is going to do tomorrow or next week or next year, I become pretty suspicious. You should, too. Pay a fortune teller for their prediction of your future love life, if you must, but never pay a financial advisor to predict the future direction of the markets.

- **MYTH #3**: *Tactical Allocation Is An Effective Way To Invest.*

> *"The Ark was built by amateurs and the Titanic by experts."*
> — Murray Cohen

Tactical allocation is the first cousin to market timing and is a favorite of the investment experts. This technique does not focus on being in or out of the *market* at the perfect time; rather, its focus is being in and out of the hot or cold *asset class* at the right time. This approach involves skewing all or a large part of one's portfolio dollars toward a particular asset class that is poised to "take off" based on macro economic conditions, a computer model, or just a hunch.

- **FACT #3**: *Tactical Allocation Is A "Fool's Errand."*

Tactical allocation has been around for decades but became especially popular after the tech bubble of 2000 burst — as in, "If only I had shifted out of tech in time!" A majority of investment professionals employ this strategy because their clients either expect or insist they use it. Too bad for both of them. For the advisor it means a short-term client relationship, and for the client it means dissatisfaction with their advisor.

Roger Gibson, author of the book *Asset Allocation*, offers up a great hypothetical scenario wherein there is a "Tactical Allocator" who has a successful system for forecasting which asset class(es) to be in and which not to be in. Gibson further assumes that they started implementing their method using the following major asset classes to move in and out of:

- Large company stocks
- Small company stocks
- Long-term bonds
- Short-term bonds

Investing $1 million in 1925, our tactical allocator would have amassed over $20 trillion by 1998. Gibson writes, "[This is] substantially more than the $13 trillion market value of all shares outstanding of all publicly traded stock in the United States — in essence, our 1925 millionaire would now own all of corporate America and approximately half of all non-U.S. companies from around the world!"

Gibson further mentions a scenario whereby a tactical asset allocator has had the use of four even broader asset classes to choose from than the previous example:

- S&P 500
- EAFE (measure of non-U.S. Stock)
- NAREIT (Index of Real Estate Investment Trusts)
- GSCI (Goldman Sachs Commodity Index)

If our tactical allocator had chosen the #1 performing asset class each year from the broad list above for a 15-year period starting in 1984, his clients would have earned a compound rate of return of 32.19%. Gibson checked the best-known database of professionally managed international and domestic mutual funds over that same time period and found that not one fund was "remotely close."

He then looked at what the results would be if a manager picked just the second best-performing asset class from the four each year. If a manager had accomplished this "not particularly impressive achievement," the compound annual return would have been 19.32%. Out of this huge database, less than 1% had a better performance than the 19.4%, and *none of them cited tactical allocation as part of their investment strategy!*

- **MYTH #4:** *Individual Stocks Outperform Stock Mutual Funds.*

> *"There are two times in a man's life when he should not speculate: when he can't afford it, and when he can."*
>
> – Mark Twain

This presumption states that because mutual funds have internal expenses (management fees), which individual stocks don't have, and because they invest in hundreds of stocks, their performance is inferior to that of a well-chosen group of individual stocks. Pundits further conclude it is foolish to invest your hard-earned money into funds due to the lack of control over the timing of taxable sales mutual funds execute.

- **FACT #4:** *Stock Mutual Funds Tend to Outperform Individual Stocks (With Less Risk).*

Let me say first that stocks can and do outperform mutual funds during selected time frames. It is, however, a misconception to believe that stocks outperform mutual funds on a regular basis. The opposite is often true.

As you can see from the performance comparison chart on page 28, the notion of individual stocks performing better than stock mutual funds is a myth over various time frames. Since we investors have a ratio of roughly three times more unhappiness with the market during downturns compared to the happiness during times of stock market gains, the "Percentage of Stocks with Negative Returns" is particularly troubling. The Percentage of Stocks with Negative Returns for the 1-Year, 3-Year, 5-Year and 10-Year periods ending December 31, 2006 is above 30%. In the most recent 1-Year and 3-Year periods, the Percentage of Stocks with Negative Returns actually approaches 40% (39.4% and 37.6%, respectively).

Now, take a look at the same category for mutual funds. The Percentage of Funds with Negative Returns is astoundingly low — from a high of 4.1% for the 5-Year period to a low of 0.6% for the 10-Year period.

STOP & THINK

U.S. Stocks as of December 31, 2006	1 Year	3 Years	5 Years	10 Years
Number of Stocks Surviving the Entire Period	6,133	5,573	5,214	3,626
Mean Equal-Weighted Annualized Return (%)	17.5	6.3	6.6	3.2
Median Annualized Return (%)	8.4	7.3	9.4	7.7
Share-Weighted Annualized Return (%)	18.5	-	-	-
Percentage of Stocks with Negative Returns (%)	39.4	37.6	32.7	31.3

U.S. Equity Funds as of December 31, 2006	1 Year	3 Years	5 Years	10 Years
Number of Funds Surviving the Entire Period	2,637	2,274	2,025	1,059
Mean Equal-Weighted Annualized Return (%)	13.2	11.1	7.5	8.8
Median Annualized Return (%)	13.4	10.8	6.9	8.5
Net Asset-Weighted Annualized Return (%)	14.4	-	-	-
Percentage of Funds with Negative Returns (%)	2.1	0.7	4.1	0.6

Source: Craig Israelsen, "Tales of the Tape." Financial Planning Magazine. March 2007, pp. 123-128

Okay, so it makes sense that a mutual fund would have less downside potential than a stock because a mutual fund has an inherent advantage of being diversified into hundreds, sometimes thousands, of stocks vs. the fate of just one stock. But one might say a mutual fund's upside potential is correspondingly curtailed because that same diversification means that ownership of poor-performing stocks can offset the fund manager's winning stocks. This supposedly leads to mediocre, market lagging returns. This is also a myth.

Look again at the performance chart comparing stocks vs. stock mutual funds. The "Median Annualized Return" for stocks in the 1-Year period is 8.4% vs. stock mutual funds' returns of 13.4%. Same story in the 3-Year period — stocks returned 7.3% while stock mutual funds made 10.8% during the same period. Stocks outperformed stock mutual funds just once during the four periods listed on the chart — the 5-Year period.

I would be the first to admit that there are periods when stocks, as a whole, outperform stock mutual funds. But the facts really do speak for themselves, at least over the last 1, 3, 5 and 10-year time frames. It is often a mistake to generalize about things, but for those who tell you that individual stocks usually perform better than stock mutual funds, you can tell them they are full of ... myth!

Now That I Know The Truth, What Am I Supposed Do? (Hint: Get A Plan!)

So far, I have spent this entire chapter presenting rebuttal data to our culture's belief in investing myths. Hopefully I have done an adequate job of convincing you that markets are not predictable and, therefore, market timing and tactical allocation are, by definition, unattainable.

> *"The will to win is worthless if you do not have the will to prepare"*
>
> – Thane Yost

If I have, then you may be saying to yourself, "What am I supposed to do?" What kind of financial advisor would I be if all I did was point out all that is wrong with the way investors invest their money and didn't offer a solution?

Here is what you should do. Here's what works.

1. **Diversify**. But it isn't just the avoidance of putting all of your eggs in one basket — you must choose the *right* baskets! This requires investing in many different asset types — stocks (international and domestic), bonds (international and domestic), REITs, commodities, etc. Choose asset classes that are not highly correlated to one another — ones that don't walk in lock step. Use at least 10 different asset classes that respond differently to the same economic environment. The best way to invest in an adequate number of asset classes is to use a mutual fund format. *Do not* use individual stocks for multi-asset class investing. It doesn't work.

2. **Have discipline**. Periodically rebalance your group of non-correlated mutual funds back to the original percentages of the overall portfolio. After all, if the portfolio has asset classes that are performing very differently from each other, then the percent each asset class represents of the total should vary greatly over time. By rebalancing periodically, you sell down some of the profits from the best-performing asset class, taking those profits and buying into those asset classes that have not performed as well, bringing them back up to their proper percent representation of the portfolio. This is a disciplined approach to an old axiom of investing that is not a myth: "Buy low, sell high."

3. **Employ reasonably priced concentrated mutual funds**. As I mentioned above, the mutual fund arrangement is the best, most efficient technique to capture the returns of an asset class. Use those that have reasonable expenses or employ an advisor who uses them. I like concentrated funds, those funds that have fewer than 100, sometimes fewer than 50 stocks, because, contrary to popular belief, I think they actually have less risk than a fund having hundreds of stocks. I embrace this principle because if I have done my job for my clients (or

you have done your own due diligence) and identified an exceptional mutual fund team, I want that team's best 50-100 ideas, not their best 300-400. If you have discovered a world-class mutual fund manager, make sure they only have 50 to 100 investment choices in their portfolio. Don't let them dilute (pollute) those great choices with mediocre choices just to accommodate more money being thrown at the fund by investors chasing performance. Studies show that when a successful fund begins to get swamped with fresh deposits from investors, they typically must expand the number of their investment choices, too. This expansion has a negative impact on their ability to continue to outperform, as their smaller extraordinary list of investment choices becomes a larger, more ordinary list. In effect, they *become the market.*

4. **Don't listen to the "noise."** Leading business economist, the late Edgar R. Fiedler said, "The herd instinct among forecasters makes sheep look like independent thinkers." Because more individuals are participating in the stock market than ever, it is only natural that the number of financial forecasters has subsequently increased—sort of like the number of lions increasing in the presence of more gazelles.

Unfortunately, forecasters get lots of media exposure, which leads to a lot of confusion and anxiety for investors due to the number of opinions by these experts who seem so very confident in their prognostications. It is when this anxiety gets to fever pitch brought on by the noise, that investors tend to make their worst investment decisions. Make it your personal mission NOT to be one of them!

Here's how to beat the noise:

1. **Once you have made a plan, stick to it**. Of course, make adjustments to it along the way, but don't scrap it all together just because some talking head says the market is going to decline tomorrow. And just because your friend or work associate did it doesn't mean you should, too. In fact, maybe you should consider taking the opposite action!

2. **Take the long-term view before you get too wound up.** If you look back at any poor decisions you have made in your life, I will bet you that they were emotionally charged. You deserve a first-rate investment plan, and a first-rate investment plan has no room for emotions. As for all that noise out there, it is only going to amplify from here. The sooner you decide that you have no room in your investment life for the noise, the better investor you will become!

3. **Consider engaging an investment advisor.** I know, this sounds a bit self-serving, but you should think about hiring one. Your financial health is just as important as your physical health, right? Sometimes you don't know you are sick until the doctor completes an exam and makes treatment recommendations. Have an investment advisor perform a *financial exam* and make recommendations. If you still have difficulty filtering out the noise, ongoing management of your money can be a viable option, too. Maybe it's time to let a trained professional worry about your portfolio.

If there is one thing I have learned in the past 25 years of counseling clients , it is this: Money alone does not bring true peace of mind, but the opposite is also true: It is difficult to have peace of mind if you have money worries.

Michael F. Booker
Financial Synergies Asset Management, Inc.
1177 West Loop South, Suite 1400
Houston, Texas 77027
713.623.6600 (tel)
www.finsyn.com

Michael Booker is a Certified Financial Planner™ (CFP®), Chartered Financial Consultant (ChFC), Certified Fund Specialist (CFS), and Board Certified in Asset Allocation (BCAA). Michael has been in the financial planning industry for more than 26 years. He was named one of "America's Top Financial Advisors" (1996-1999, 2001, and 2002) by *Worth Magazine*, one of "The Ten Most Dependable Wealth Managers" by Goldline Research (2006 and 2007), and included on Consumers' Research Council's "Guide To America's Top Financial Planners" (2005 and 2006) Michael has been a guest speaker in national and local shows including Biz Radio's "Money Smart" and Fox network's "Fox on Money."

3. RISK: It's a Personal Thing

Scott Johnson, CFP®, CIMA
Johnson, O'Brien & Toomer LLC

Two friends walk into a brokerage office with $100,000 to invest. One friend buys municipal bonds and the other buys emerging market stocks. Although the two friends may have identical financial positions, they obviously feel differently about risk. After all, risk is a very personal thing.

Not only can risk be viewed differently, it can be measured differently as well. However, one thing most investors have in common is their concern about losing money on investments. Losses occur when the total return (capital gains or capital loss plus dividends and interest) is less than the original amount invested — not much disagreement there.

In addition to risking investment loss, an investor also runs the risk of sub-standard returns. Although not a loss, poor performance is not desirable either. However, for purposes of this discussion, we shall focus on traditional losses. Later in the chapter, we will also discuss risk tolerance levels, investment portfolio risks and developing risk profiles.

The Standard & Poor's 500 Index has averaged around 10%, for the past 25 years (Vanguard S&P

500 Index). So anyone who invests in the S&P Index can reasonably expect to receive a return of 10% in any given year. That doesn't mean he will get it, but he can reasonably expect he will. Actually, the S&P Index seldom returns 10% in any given year. It is usually greater than or less than 10% and the average, or mean, is around 10%. But like the fellow in the kitchen who has one hand in the freezer and one hand on the stove, the average may not be of much comfort if the extremes are too great.

Volatility Around the Expected Return

Broadly speaking, volatility refers to the degree of unpredictable change over time of a certain variable (typically short-term). If your portfolio gets a return of 10% annually with little or no fluctuation around the 10%, you should be pretty happy. Unfortunately, high returns don't cluster around the expected return in any given year. The S&P Index has had annual returns over 30% and losses of more than 20% in any given year (Vanguard S&P 500 Index). Only if an investor held the S&P Index stocks for a long period of time, such as 25 years, would his return be closely reflective of the expected 10%.

> **Even though investors can't control volatility in stocks, *they can control the volatility in their accounts*. They can do that by moving money from risky investments to ones less risky.**

During the second half of the 1990s, the S&P Index averaged more than 27% returns for each of the years 1995-1999. The next three-year period, 2000–2003, the S&P Index dropped nearly 40%. The NASDAQ stocks fell around 70%. What a ride! But it wasn't much fun for those who took it. So to get that long-term return of 10% in stocks, an investor may have to put up with nerve-racking volatility.

Even though investors can't control volatility in stocks, they can help control the volatility in their accounts. They can do that by moving money from risky investments to those less risky. Of course, by shifting money from stocks to short-term bonds, for example, the long-term investment return will be lower. However, consider this: If an investor invests $100,000 and loses 50%, he has to earn 100% on the remaining $50,000 to break even the next year. To put it another way, if he loses 50% he must earn 10% a year for the next seven years to recoup most of his loss. Yes, controlling losses is important.

Standard Deviation

Measuring the risk of an investment is normally accomplished with standard deviation, a statistical tool used to measure volatility around an expected outcome. (See graph below.)

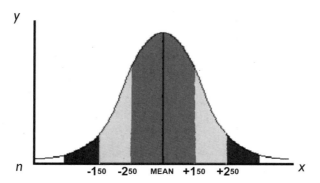

Don't let your eyes get glossy, it's not that bad. All standard deviation does is take a sampling of events and see how two-thirds of them cluster around their average. For example, if we determine the average return of the S&P 500 is 10% over the last 20 years, standard deviation would tell us the maximum and minimum returns around that 10% which would include or explain 67% of the returns. If standard deviation were 15, we could expect two-thirds of the future returns to come in between a -5% and a +25%.

Standard deviation is computed by finding the average, calculating each year's variance from the average or mean, squaring them to eliminate the negatives, totaling the squared variances, dividing their summation by the number of observations, and finally, taking the square root of the result.

Fortunately, standard deviation is often computed for you. It's important to understand how it works, though, because the investment industry uses it to measure risks. What is often missed or misunderstood is that standard deviation does not explain all the risks with regard to investments. Remember, standard deviation only measures volatility. There will be times, especially during periods where stocks are trading away from their long-term growth trend line, when standard deviation does not explain all the risks. Regression to the mean risk is not fully captured by standard deviation. (There will be more on this later.)

Another thing to keep in mind is the time period during which standard deviation was calculated. Standard deviation is often calculated for one, three, and five-year or longer time periods. Shorter time periods can be misleading. Try to use data over longer time frames for standard deviation.

How to Use Standard Deviation

If you could get a 10% return with one investment (A) that has a standard deviation of 3% and another investment (B) with a standard deviation of 15%, which one would you choose? Of course, you would choose (A) the one with the lower standard deviation because it has less fluctuation around the expected return. Not only does it provide more predictability, it is also more liquid should you have to sell. Everything else being equal, choose the investment with the lower standard deviation — its lower risk.

Of course, there will be stock opportunities with high standard deviations and you may want to invest in them. Just make sure you are taking the risk appropriate for you in your overall investment portfolio. You can also reduce the standard deviation in your investment portfolio by reducing correlation. Stocks that move together are correlated, like oil stocks being influenced by a changing price of crude oil. Investments that move in opposite directions are negatively correlated. If you could match up all your investments where they would be negatively correlated, you could theoretically reduce your risk to 0.

That is a very difficult thing to do. However, you still can reduce risk by being less than 100% correlated. You could own a stock in the oil industry and a stock in the airline industry, for example. Although not negatively correlated, they certainly would not react similarly to changes in the price of oil. Even if each stock had a standard deviation of 15%, together their combined standard deviation would probably be less than 15%. That's why you should diversify — to reduce correlation and the portfolio's standard deviation. Of course, even diversification cannot eliminate the risk of fluctuating prices and uncertain returns.

Let's return to a point made earlier; standard deviation does not explain all the risks. During the second half of the 1990s, the S&P 500 averaged more than 27% returns, yet the standard deviation during that time period was less than 7%. Of course, the standard deviation *used* during those years was more like 15-18% (even that was too low). The point is this: Did investors really believe the S&P 500 would continue to have returns of 27%, or more

— with a standard deviation suggesting the downside risk was no worse than a 12% return (27% expected return minus 15% standard deviation)?

As mentioned before, during the next three years, 2000-2002, the S&P 500 fell 40%. The NASDAQ (over-the-counter market) plummeted 70%. Clearly, standard deviation did not account for these huge losses. Yes, the losses occurred out on the tails of the normal distribution curve (outside of one standard deviation), but that doesn't mean they were unavoidable.

What were the additional risks not explained by standard deviation? One important risk is called the regression to the mean. Regression to the mean is the tendency of extreme results to revert back to the norm. It doesn't apply for random results, but stock moves are not random. So, the regression to the mean risk does apply to stocks. Even if earnings of the underlying companies were growing 27% to generate average annual stock increases of 27%, could those earnings be expected to continue growing at that rate? The answer is no. The new economy still had to abide by the old rules of supply and demand.

The regression to the mean risk is just that. It does not predict a change in stock prices. It only adjusts the risk. Be very clear on this. No attempt is made here to predict returns. In the 1990s when stocks were rising rapidly, regression to the mean risks were also rising, but that only meant stock prices had a tendency to revert back to more normal valuations after periods of over-performance. Stocks, after all, do reflect the earnings of their underlying companies. On occasion, stock prices can — and do — trade away from company valuations, but at some point stock prices will re-align themselves with company valuations. Just remember, stock prices and company valuations can be matched and still have a RTM risk if they are above their long-term growth trend lines.

When a stock maven says stocks are appropriately valued, does he mean according to the earnings or to the long-term growth trend line?

Not only do stock prices trade with aberrant behavior, company earnings can also be erratic. So stock prices can be accurately valued according to company earnings, but what if the company earnings themselves are unsustainable like they were in the 1990s?

STOP & THINK

One might be tempted to assume an investor who reduced his stock positions as prices moved higher was wrong because he missed out on higher profits later. But if he were managing his risk properly, how could he be wrong? He isn't according to the industry's interpretation of regulatory guidance (NASD). They have determined that the risks must match the investor, not the returns. Keep your risks managed properly.

Risk Profile

All investors should develop a risk profile for themselves. If you work with a financial advisor, he could create one for you.

The risk profile is independent of how you feel about risk. It utilizes financial data or information to define your financial profile. Once the financial profile is established an appropriate risk level can be quantified for you. That quantified level will be in terms of standard deviation.

Let's take a look at some of the items to consider when creating the risk profile:

- Age
- Spouse information
- Income
- Expenses
- Size of family
- Educational needs for children
- Insurance
- Savings and investments
- Health (special needs)
- Goals and objectives

The list is not limited to the above items, but notice all we are concerned with at this point is non-emotional facts and figures. You want to have an unbiased evaluation of your financial picture. It is important for you and your advisor to determine what risk level you *should* take. Once the appropriate standard deviation for you is determined you can move on to the next step.

Risk Tolerance Level

The risk tolerance level is totally separate from the risk profile in that it ignores financial facts and is solely concerned with your emotional side. How do you feel about risk? At what level of risk can you sleep at night?

You may get asked to fill out a risk questionnaire designated to develop a psychological profile of yourself. It might include questions like, "how would you feel if your account dropped 20%". The questionnaire is helpful in ferreting out emotional responses to risk.

It also helps develop a quantifiable risk tolerance level. How do we quantify the risk tolerance level? You guessed it — standard deviation.

You will want the standard deviation of the Risk Tolerance Level to match that of the Risk Profile. Sometimes they don't match. The fellow with kids in college, a mortgage and a limited budget who gambles away his money at the casino is an example. Here is where your financial advisor might go through an educational process with you. Often an investor does not fully understand the consequences of changes in the market and how those changes can affect the risk he is taking.

The asset allocation in a portfolio will reflect market changes in varying degrees. For example, if an investor has 80% bonds, 20% stocks, he should expect to lose only 2% in his stock portfolio if the overall market drops 10%. The stock allocation of the portfolio will have an impact on how the portfolio reacts to market changes.

> *Once you have risk profile (standard deviation) equal to risk tolerance level (standard deviation), all you have to do is put together a portfolio that has a standard deviation equal to that of risk profile and the risk tolerance level.*

This is a good place to interject a few comments on risk management.

Let's take a couple who walk into a brokerage office with $500,000 from the husband's IRA rollover. Over his wife's strenuous objections he puts all the money on a long call option. He doubles his money and tells his wife, "See I told you so." Was he right? No, the husband got lucky. He took an inappropriate risk. Now let's look at the time period between 1995 and 1999. An investor has money in technology stocks. As the techs rise, he lets his money ride until he has 80% of his portfolio in technology because technology stocks outperformed the old economy stocks. At the height of the market he sold, thereby quadrupling his money in four years. Was he right? No, he got lucky. Don't manage your risks with luck.

Portfolios should be risk driven. Look for investments designed to help maximize your return within your risk limits, but make sure the overall portfolio is risk driven.

Investment Portfolio Risks

Now that you have determined the risk level to take, just make sure you are taking the same risk level in your portfolio. Often an interview process will go like this: A client says he wants to retire with $2 million in his account, and the broker informs him he must invest aggressively to meet his goal. The account might be invested in all, or almost all, stocks, with a large portion in small cap or emerging market stocks. Everything is arranged so that the projections show the investor will meet his goals upon retirement. Then some time later, the account plummets.

Don't let goal-setting manage your risk. If you don't care about risk, why not set your goals higher — like a billion dollars? Get the point? Asset allocation software programs are important tools for constructing an investment portfolio. Too bad they aren't used more responsibly. Many portfolios are put together without allowing risk management to be the main driver. But why determine the risk profile and the risk tolerance level if they are not used when building the portfolio? Risk should drive the portfolio right down to each investment purchased.

> Don't let goal-setting manage your risk. If you don't care about risk, why not set your goals higher… like a $ billion. Get the point?

Two risk management problems in asset allocation models are chasing performance and ignoring regression to the mean risk. They are actually related. An asset class that outperforms in any year has an increased risk of underperforming the following year. Once a portfolio is in place, annual re-balancing mitigates the problem, but not entirely. Chasing performance happens when a novice investor picks out the asset classes or stocks that outperformed in a prior year and loads up the portfolio with those picks. Odds are the portfolio may be doomed. (That strategy seldom works; the laws of supply and demand tend to bring out-performers back to normality.)

Regression to the mean risk is a problem because it is not fully accounted for in the standard deviation calculations. Standard deviation only shows historical volatility around the expected return. It does not explain the regression risk. Almost all allocation software programs account for risk with standard deviation, regardless whether they use historical data or the Monte Carlo method. Both miss the regression to the mean risk. You will need to adjust standard deviation with a regression to the mean factor, so if the market, asset class, or stock is trading above its long-term growth trend line (LT-GTL), do the adjustment. A rule of thumb adjustment is to calculate how far the security or market is trading above or below its long-term growth trend line, and then adjust the standard deviation by that amount. For example, if a stock is 20% above its LTGTL, multiply the stock's standard deviation by 1.2 times. By doing that you raise its standard deviation and you will have to reduce the dollars you put into the stock to stay within the overall standard deviation of the portfolio. Conversely, if a stock is trading below its LTGTL, you can add money to that stock. This adjustment can be made for the market, asset class or security. Once you do the adjustment, the risk management parts fit together nicely. The risk you should take equals the risk you feel you want to take equals the risk you do take.

> Risk Profile Standard Deviation = Risk Tolerance Level Standard Deviation = Portfolio Standard Deviation
>
> *Or, if needed;*
>
> Risk Profile Standard Deviation = Risk Tolerance Level Standard Deviation = Portfolio (Return to the Mean Adjusted) Standard Deviation

Summary

Now you have managed the risks. You may want to go after the highest return you can get within your risk limits. Let risk drive the portfolio. Use risk to evaluate the market's asset classes and individual securities. Once you have run the asset allocation program to maximize return within your risk level, check to see if you need to adjust for a regression to the mean risk. Apply the needed adjustments and re-allocate. You don't necessarily need to eliminate potential investment candidates, just adjust your purchase amount to match the risk level you want to take. Risk management should permeate the portfolio. Buy what you want to buy; however, let risk tell you how much to buy. Use this technique to re-balance your portfolio as well. Generally, annual rebalancing will do, but you should work with your financial advisor to establish a time frame that works for your specific situation. And always re-member that asset allocation cannot eliminate the risk of fluctuating prices and uncertain returns.

Managing your portfolio according to risk won't allow you to double your portfolio in 60 days, but then, chances are you won't sustain devastating loss-es either. Getting a good return within your risk level should be your goal.

Presley S. Johnson
Johnson, O'Brien & Toomer LLC
Investment Management Group
4021 Meadows Lane, Suite B
Las Vegas, NV 89107
702.853.7318. or 888.267.5072 (tel)
psjohnson@wachoviafinet.com

Presley Scott Johnson is managing principal for Johnson, O'Brien & Toomer, a full-service stock brokerage firm in Las Vegas, Nevada that offers a full line of investment products through Wachovia Securities.

Scott has been in the brokerage industry since 1975 when he started as a financial consultant for Dean Witter. He worked for 30 years as a broker with three major Wall Street firms before starting his own business in 2005.

Scott attended Tennessee Technological University and University of Nevada Las Vegas and he holds a Bachelor of Science degree in finance and Master of Business Administration. He also is a Certified Financial Planner™ (CFP®) and a Certified Investment Management Analyst (CIMA). Scott is married with two children and lives in Las Vegas.

4. Protecting Your Assets and Lifestyle from Catastrophic Medical Expenses

Amy Rose Herrick, ChFC, IAR

I magine the following conversation takes place at a restaurant between two women having lunch: "Emily, I'm so grateful for all the help you have given me," says Susan, an obvious long-time friend. "The offer of a loan is appreciated but even with the money my folks could give me, we will still lose our home. I have been selling assets, including the second car, to bring some type of money in for us. With the foreclosure costs, I doubt we will see one cent of the house sale proceeds. My credit is gone with all the missed or late payments and I am really worried about finding a place to live. I've spent every dime of savings."

She continues, "In an attempt to make minimum payments, keep the utilities on, and keep some food on the table while I tried to get well, I took credit card cash advances until they were maxed out. The doctors say that I'll be off work for at least another six months to finish treatment and recover my health. I hope I have a job to go back to, but after being gone almost a year altogether, that possibility looks pretty grim too."

Susan, obviously very troubled and wiping away a silent tear, goes on to say to her friend, "With all the

Surge in Bankruptcies

There have been numerous studies conducted to determine why there are so many filed bankruptcies. Most occur when one's income is diminished or a disabling health condition occurs. According to a study done by Project: HOPE, The People-to-People Health Foundation, Inc., half cited medical reasons for filing. Said the report, *"In 2001, 1.458 million American families filed for bankruptcy. To investigate medical contributors to bankruptcy, we surveyed 1,771 personal bankruptcy filers in five federal courts and subsequently completed in-depth interviews with 931 of them. About half cited medical causes, which indicates that 1.9–2.2 million Americans (filers plus dependents) experienced medical bankruptcy. Among those whose illnesses led to bankruptcy, out-of-pocket costs averaged $11,854 since the start of illness; 75.7 percent had insurance at the onset of illness. Medical debtors were 42 percent more likely than other debtors to experience lapses in coverage. Even middle-class insured families often fall prey to financial catastrophe when sick.[1]"* These are frightening statistics.

1 www.healthaffairs.org

problems in front of me, I know that I need to talk to an attorney about filing bankruptcy. Do you think if I file bankruptcy I will lose my team of doctors? I am already in debt to them and owe thousands of dollars. A few months ago I thought having a good job, savings and some health insurance was enough, but now I know it isn't. I'm scared. What do I do now?"

Emily had no idea how to respond to Susan. She wanted to help, but nothing short of a miracle could save her friend from impending financial disaster.

Susan is losing almost everything she worked so hard for over the years and can do little to stop it. At this point, it's like being on a roller coaster, and she's along for the ride. Sometimes, for people in Susan's situation, bankruptcy is the only recourse. (See Surge in Bankruptcies.)

What Susan is facing is not uncommon. All one has to do is read the paper, watch the news or listen to a friend who knows someone facing a financial crisis to hear about such circumstances. Unfortunately, many of these individuals are without adequate savings, investments, and insurance benefits.

If Susan had a crystal ball just few months earlier, do you think she may have made some minor changes in her lifestyle that included setting aside some of her income for more comprehensive insurance planning?

Chapter 4. Catastrophic Medical Expenses

Prudent planning tells us to build an emergency savings cushion. The ideal primary accumulation vehicles in most households would be liquid, non-fluctuating accounts such as savings accounts, money markets or short-duration CDs for reserves totaling three to six months' of gross income. If you are a small business owner or are self-employed, you may need to have larger liquid cash reserves to pay ongoing operating expenses of your business for similar time periods.

Here are some sad facts that should motivate you to act now:

- In the last 10 minutes 390 Americans became disabled. Thirty percent of all employees in the U.S. between the ages of 35-65 will suffer a disability and will be out of work at least 90 days.[2]

- The Health Association of America determined one in seven of all employees in the United States will be disabled for five years at some point in their lives. Is it really accurate to believe it couldn't happen to you? Sadly, some of you who are reading this now will not have the same job or the old homestead to go back to when you are recuperating after a medical crisis occurs.

- Nearly 48% of all personal mortgage foreclosures are income and health related.[3]

Milliman, a leading national insurance actuarial and product development firm, reported in May of 2007 that a "typical" insured family of four in the U.S. will spend $14,500 in 2007 on medical care. An amount of $5,591 represented the out-of-pocket costs for the family. The rest were premiums paid by the employer. That was a 8.4% increase over 2006! Overall, medical costs have increased an average of 9.3% annually the last five years, so is it reasonable to hope that the inflationary trend will decrease? I believe that whether you are single or have a family, you need to plan for budget increases in health care costs.

It Really is all About Money (and Time) and Time Really is Money

Expenses for normal everyday life won't simply go away. What really happens in an emergency like this? The bills do not pay themselves and don't forget there are the crisis figures, too. This is money that you must have for additional expenses in times of need. Everyone around you seems to be af-

---

2 Nationl Safety Council
3 Norton Bankruptcy Advisor 2000

fected. Consider the following:

- You need to continue paying your mortgage or rent payments.
- You need to pay for essential utilities like electricity, water, phone and gas for comfort and healing.
- You must buy food and beverages to survive.

Expenses can escalate even faster if you have a family member taking time off work to help with your medical treatments or transportation to and from appointments. Do you need to replace their lost wages too? Some people can use the Family Medical Leave Act, available to employees who need to assist family members. This benefit will protect their employment, but it is unpaid leave in almost every instance. A disability may require the spouse or adult child who may be caring for you to spend less time at work. This could lead to a reduction of a second person's wages. The financial implications affect everyone.

An often forgotten consideration is the affected employers. They have businesses to run. How long can they afford to keep you, your spouse or adult child at a reduced schedule or hold a position vacant in order to help you?

There is so much to consider if you become disabled. Where will your income come from? Do you own a personal disability insurance plan? Does your employer have a short- or long-term disability insurance plan for the employees via payroll deduction? Normally, all of these plans will replace no more than 60-70% of your pre-disability income. If you are paying the premiums, the benefits are usually not included in your taxable income. If the employer is paying the premium, then the benefits usually are taxable income.

When do your benefits start? Like a payroll check, you must earn the benefit before it is paid. If you have a 90-day waiting period, you probably won't see the first check until 120 to 150 days after your disability date. How will you pay your bills during that four- to five-month lag time? What is the maximum number of payments you could expect, or at what age will they cease?

Six Steps to Take Now to Protect Yourself and Your Assets

How can you avoid being a financially devastated statistic like Susan? Simple: Here is a six-part income and asset protection solution designed to control your out-of-pocket costs, limit your overall financial exposure, reduce your income taxes, provide an income stream in times of illness or injury, and secure real peace of mind for yourself and your family.

Step #1: Various Health Plans. If you do not have a good group health plan, secure a qualified health savings account (HSA) that pays 100% of covered expenses after the deductible is met. At this writing, this could limit a single person's medical expense exposure to $2,850 (adjusted annually), or a family's medical expense exposure to $5,650 (adjusted annually) regardless of the number of family members (at least two) covered by the plan. If you are between the ages of 55-64, you can add an additional $800 annually. Couples with both spouses between ages 55-64 can double this amount for up to an additional $1,600 more a year.

> So you have a group health plan? Great! However, if you are off work, how long can you continue your health coverage? When are the premium payments due to your employer? How much will the new monthly premiums be during the time you are separated without the employer contributions?

I recommend that you compare the costs of securing private portable health insurance coverage to the costs of available employer sponsored group coverage if participation is not mandatory. In many cases, group coverage is not a bargain, as when the overall group has a high claim history and you do not. Ask a qualified agent to compare plans and shop the coverage for you. Know what is best for your financial situation and your coverage needs.

Are you without coverage now and believe you are uninsurable due to pre-existing conditions? Contact your state insurance commissioner to determine what your state-guaranteed issue options are and apply. These guaranteed issue plans will not be inexpensive, and there may be some limits on coverage available. However, the treatment you may need without coverage will likely be much more expensive, or unobtainable. Why? Because according to a recent paper by Gerard Anderson, a professor at Johns Hopkins University, the uninsured paid more than twice as much as those with negotiated insurance plans that more closely follow the Medicare allowable cost levels.

If you are concerned about the possibility of an accident causing you to reach your high deductible quickly, and this holds you back from the higher deductible health insurance plan associated with an HSA or state pool, there may be a type of additional coverage you could consider. There are some remarkably low-cost plans available that pay benefits *only* for accidental medical or dental expenses, from $1,000-$5,000 per occurrence. This complements your health insurance and is not a replacement for it. Does the potential policy benefit, over time, warrant the premiums required for a policy that will pay for accidental medical or dental expenses *only*? Determine what makes sense for you.

Step #2: Prescription Medicine Discounts. Take advantage of discounts and special savings on prescription medicine. One way of doing this is by going to www.kansasdrugcard.com to receive your pre-activated personal discount prescription drug cards. These cards are available absolutely free. Yes, they are free. Although it says Kansas in the Web site title, these instantly available online discount drug cards can be used nationwide, in two different large networks of pharmacies with names you will quickly recognize. You print the cards yourself after filling in your name and email address. No income qualifying, no medical questions or other personal information is required! The site has a link to locate a list of participating pharmacies in your area from both networks, and separate links to compare medication pricing among participating pharmacies.

If you have private prescription coverage, compare the cost of filling the prescription with your group or private insurance card and this discount card. You can fill the prescription with whichever is the lowest cost option. Take into account your medication needs on an ongoing basis and determine if there is an advantage to having the costs of the prescription counted toward the deductible to your plan. These cards are not a replacement for health insurance, they are a complement to any other prescription coverage you currently have in place. If you do not have prescription coverage, this card could help reduce your prescription costs up to 75%.

Step #3: Health Savings Accounts and Employer Sponsored Pre-Tax Plans. If you choose an HSA, fund the tax-deductible HSA to the maximum allowed by law to have tax-free monies ready to pay medical expenses as you need them. This pre-planning saves you money by lowering your federal (and, if it applies, state) income tax bills.

If you use a group plan instead of an HSA, set aside the maximum out-of-pocket liability in a liquid account you can access if/when needed. If your employer offers a pre-tax plan, learn how to use it! What is your annual maximum out-of-pocket limit on your health insurance for covered services (including deductibles and co-pays) in addition to your premiums? $2,000? $10,000? $20,000 or more? How much is enough for your situation?

Step #4: Critical Illness and Key Man Insurance. Purchase a critical illness product that is triggered to pay a $50,000-$500,000 tax-free lump sum cash benefit upon any one of 15-20-plus occurrences, such as heart attack, stroke, cancer, or blindness. You generally choose the amount you would like to apply for. The policy will go through underwriting, just like most other insurance coverage to determine if you qualify. I suggest you apply to replace two years of wages. Within two years of the initial medical issue, there should be enough time to see what lifestyle changes need to be implemented by the household if the situation is permanent, whether you will be cured or, in all likelihood, at least be able to go back to work in some capacity

> *A critical illness only policy is not a replacement for health insurance. It is a complement to the coverage you already have.*

Do you own a business? This type of policy can be used in a business arrangement to quickly infuse cash into your business in the event a business partner or a key employee has a disabling illness. Why would a business want to pay for that kind of coverage? These funds can keep a business viable until the missing partner or key employee is able to return to full-time employment, or perhaps allow enough breathing room for the business to be sold to someone else instead of imploding. You may want to have an agreement in place to continue pre-disability wages for a time. Remember, if you deduct the premiums as a business expense, then all the proceeds will be taxable income to the recipient. Talk to your accountant and tax professional about paying these business premiums with non-deductible dollars.

Step #5: Long-Term Care and Disability Insurance. For adults nearing the end of the working years consider the purchase of a long-term Care (LTC) policy that pays cash benefits if you become unable to care for yourself because of a loss of functional capacity or other cognitive loss such as Alzheimer's disease.

All or a portion of LTC premiums could be income-tax deductible if you meet tax guidelines. Many states give tax breaks to residents who purchase LTC policies. Bring the amount you pay for premiums to the attention of your tax professional when you file your income taxes each year.

Younger workers should consider securing an individual disability plan to provide a disability income stream. Depending on your age or occupation, benefits may be payable to age 65. Disability premiums are not tax-deductible.

You may be able to secure either LTC or disability coverage at work. Read the coverage parameters carefully. Not all plans are portable, which means if you leave your employer or if they decide to terminate the plan, you cannot continue the coverage. If you have a pre-existing condition, securing replacement coverage may not be possible when an old policy is terminated or allowed to lapse.

Many employer-sponsored disability plans favor low-wage earners with short periods of income replacement of up to 70% of wages during a loss. For example, there could be a $2,000 maximum benefit per month, only payable for six months. The same group policy may not be an adequate short-term monthly benefit for the higher-wage earners in the same company, because the maximum policy limits may only replace a small fraction of their earnings. It is possible to have great or even excellent short-term coverage at work and very bad or poor long-term coverage (or vice versa). High-wage earners may need to have at least two coordinated policies in place to replace 60-70% of their income, and most insurers limit policy maximum coverage liability to $7,000-$10,000 per person, per month. A high-wage earner may need to implement a combination of disability and LTC policies.

How much is enough coverage for either LTC or disability insurance? An experienced agent will examine each individual situation taking into account existing employer-sponsored options, cash resources, occupation, age and your preferences to design your coverage package.

Step #6: Crisis Cash Plan. Set aside an emergency cash cushion at least equal to your elimination period on your LTC or disability plan. Some creative ways to help reach this goal (until you build the actual cash reserve amount) could be to earmark a portion of cash values in permanent life insurance, or Roth IRA contributions (not earnings), mentally earmark an investment account, identify an asset that could be sold quickly, or whatever you need to do to know where the short-term funds are going to come from. Make sure your most likely caretakers also know your plan.

Small business owners and the self-employed will need to identify or set aside additional working capital resources. This allows their businesses to continue operations with a minimal of interruptions to day-to-day operations.

Is This Type of Asset Protection Structuring Affordable?

Absolutely yes! I have examined instances where the costs of the current group health insurance premiums alone are more than the cost of this income and asset protection strategy secured on an individual basis. (See the case study on page 57 for a comprehensive example.)

This type of total income and asset protection approach is a great idea to take to your human resources department as an alternative to consider developing instead of the traditional in-force group low-deductible policy arrangements. These types of non-traditional approaches can be extremely effective when a business is attempting to improve coverage options to attract or retain key employees. In many cases, these types of coordinated plans have been used to control the double-digit spiraling benefit costs businesses are faced with at each renewal on traditional plans.

Long-Term Care Insurance Examined

According to industry statistics, 58% of group long term care (LTC) claimants are under age 65. Surprised? The top five claims were for cancer (30%), stroke (10%), with the remainder a mixture of ailments including neurological disease, dementia and multiple sclerosis. Such ailments at a younger age no longer mean dying, but they do mean disability, and a long-term disability in many, if not most, cases.

The typical group LTC claim lasted more than a year with the average claimant a young 53 years old. A startling 15% of claimants were under the age of 45. Fortunately 66% of claimants were able to receive care at home, while 17% needed more expensive care in a nursing home setting.

The good news is, we are living longer than prior generations. If you were born just 100 years ago, your life expectancy was only an average age of 47. A child born today has a life expectancy average of 78 years, an increase of about 20 years since 1929. With that good news comes some bad news from the federal Office of Personnel Management (OPM). This group determined in 2003 that a sobering 60% of the population will need some type of LTC. Planning to max out your 401(k) or have the house paid off before age 65 probably won't be sufficient planning. Only a fraction of the identified 'at risk' 60% of the population expected to incur LTC expenses has taken any action to secure LTC insurance. The majority of those in the age bracket of 45-64 have not factored this potentially huge liability into their financial plans either before or after retirement.

STOP & THINK

More sobering news is that the average cost for a year in an assisted living facility is $34,860. If one needs an upgrade to a nursing home environment, the cost soars to an average of $74,095 a year. That figure does not include time off work for your much needed support person (who is most likely a spouse or an adult child already in agony over your situation), nor does it include transportation or other incidental expenses.

Consider the results of this report: A comprehensive study by Milliman, Inc. concluded that for the majority of individuals insured, a three-year benefit may be enough for LTC coverage. Why? Only eight in 100 claimants exhausted their three-year policy benefits. Will you be in the minority or the majority? No one knows.

The No. 1 objection to buying LTC is the perception that it costs too much. The key to affording peace of mind is to design a plan that complements what other resources you already have in place.

Types of LTC Coverage

Traditional Plan. A traditional reimbursement plan pays much like your health insurance. You should be warned that someone must devote a lot of time to keep track of every medical-related expense, and that person must also be diligent in submitting each and every day's worth of costs for consideration and reimbursement. Some exhausted family members say that managing care giving, submitting claims to all involved insurers and managing payments for all the services provided is more than a full-time job.

Cash Benefit Plan. The second type of LTC insurance is a cash benefit policy. It pays cash benefits if you cannot perform two adult daily living activities (ADLs). This type of insurance is much simpler to deal with in every way. You don't need to prove how you are spending the money. A check simply arrives once a month. This type of policy dramatically lessens the headaches, time and bookkeeping burden on caregivers by eliminating the need to keep track of the submissions, reimbursement, payment and reconciliation steps.

Important Documents You Need

Document #1: Durable Power of Attorney. You need to have this important document in place so that pending personal and business issues can continue without you through your representative. I suggest you go three levels deep on these types of documents. Make your first choice, then select a second and a third choice, in case the preferred person cannot serve in that capacity at the time you really need them. Make sure copies are in the possession of all the persons listed. Be specific. Do not list "my brother Bill Smith." Include full name, address, work, cell and home phone numbers and email address — any and all ways this person can be found, and contacted quickly in an emergency.

Document #2: Medical Directive. What do you want to happen to you in a medical crisis? If you want an armed guard to keep family members away from a ventilator plug and want every known medical method applied to keep you alive, put it in print. On the other hand, if you desire no heroic efforts, or for religious reasons you do not want blood transfusions, or you desire that your organs, skin, bones or any other part of your body be used for transplants or medical science, write it down. Don't just tell someone assuming they can honor your wishes in times of crisis, write it down and pass out copies!

Document #3: Updated Will. If you do not recover, do not leave an additional mess of an estate that has to be sorted out and settled based on existing state laws to your grieving survivors. Do potential executors have copies, or is this very important document hidden somewhere that no one (besides you) will find it? Make it easy on your loved ones.

Document #4: List of Insurance Policies and Coverage. Make sure you include policy numbers and contact numbers. In the event of an emergency, a spouse or other representative may need to refer and activate many plans in a timely manner or you may lose the benefits you earned and paid for. Include life, health and accident plans, group coverage, disability policies, LTC, etc. Again, pass out copies!

Special Considerations: Physically and Developmentally Disabled Family Members

In many families, one person coordinates the ongoing care of a child or an adult with disabilities. In these cases, the primary caregiver needs to leave information and instructions for their replacement in case of the caretaker's medical crisis or death.

First, identify who will be responsible for the disabled family member if the current primary care person is no longer able to do so. Speak frankly to anyone you consider for this responsibility to determine if they are willing and, most important, able to take over this responsibility. It is better for someone to be honest and say 'no' now if they cannot handle this, rather than later when it was assumed they would be taking over. Secure at least three different possibilities so your loved one is never in the hands of the courts looking for a care solution.

Compile a letter of intent that is coordinated with a future guardian, if that becomes necessary. Draft a guide for your replacement including everything that a future guardian would need to know to transition the situation with minimal stress for everyone involved. What is the exact diagnosis or condition, what testing has been done, where are the medical records, what are the likes, dislikes, allergies, medication schedules, local pharmacy number, regularly scheduled activities, insurance information, etc? Include the daily schedule if that is critical to the care and comfort of the loved one, especially if that would help a new caregiver step in and take over easily and efficiently. It would be very helpful to include names and numbers of any respite care providers you have used in the past who know your situation and would be a good resource to call for help in a crisis.

If you have not already done so, you need to set up a special needs trust to provide a safety net beyond Social Security and Medicaid for this special family member. If you are not familiar with these types of planning tools, special needs trusts (when properly designed) will not count as available resources when it comes time to determine eligibility for any type of government-sponsored financial aid. Once the trust is in place, you should make it a priority to update all or a portion of your beneficiary designations on your retirement accounts, company benefits, and life insurance policies naming the trust, and not the disabled family member as the beneficiary. Other family members may contribute to this trust if desired.

In most cases, if your loved one has as little as $2,000 in his or her name, they may be ineligible to receive any benefits until the assets are exhausted and what they were spent on has been documented. This is not likely the scenario you had in mind. Any proceeds left in the trust at their death would go to the beneficiaries listed in the trust documents at inception. It is common to distribute unused trust assets to other family members or a favorite charity after the death of the disabled loved one when the trust is no longer needed.

Have you established legal guardianship? Parents won't have an automatic say in the care of a minor child, nor will they have access to medical records after he or she turns 18. By retaining legal guardianship of a disabled family member at any time, families can put in place tools such as trusts and limited access to bank accounts and investments to protect loved ones from people who don't have his or her best interests at heart.

Health insurance continuation after the retirement or death of the primary policyholder must be planned in advance. In most cases, disabled minor children are covered under their parents' group health insurance plan until they are no longer employed with that company, if the disability occurred before the 22nd birthday. Let your human resources officer and the insurance companies know which insured is disabled to make sure they stay covered. If the child will lose coverage because of a separation, know in advance what other options need to be applied for and secured within 30 days of separation so there is no gap in coverage. Remember to contact your state insurance commissioner for guaranteed insurability options in your state.

Documents should be distributed to family members, physicians, trust officers and anyone else who may be called on in an emergency to help with a guardian transition.

> *You must also involve a competent, caring attorney in your family affairs. This is not a luxury; this is a necessity.*

Special Considerations: Cohabitating Couples

For the first time in census history, the minority of households consist of married couples. Of the total population, 111 million households (50.2%) are in some other type of living arrangements. Non-family households amounted to 37 million individuals who are living in relationships that are not marriage-based. This group is probably the least protected medically and financially in the event of a separation, medical crisis or death of a partner.

Any rights you desire need to be created using legal documents such as wills, living wills, advance medical directives, including what non-family members can visit you, a domestic partner agreement, parenting agreement, revocable living trusts, life insurance trusts, and durable powers-of-attorney for finances, to name some of the most common ones needed.

The percentage of births to cohabitating couples is at an all-time high according to a report by research firm Child Trends. A whopping 52% of births to single women in 2001 (the most recent data available) occurred in live-in relationships. Has paternity been firmly established? What about any future Social Security benefits for any children born outside of marriage? Here is an example of what is in jeopardy for the surviving parent when a 35-year-old father becomes disabled and then dies without establishing paternity on his child. Before disability, he had been earning a $65,000 annual wage that was supporting the household. The child and surviving parent could be ineligible or hindered from collecting up to approximately $921 in monthly disability benefits, or up to approximately $2,764 in monthly survivor benefits.

What about health insurance for children of non-married partners? If coverage is work- related is it convertible to individual policies and, if so, what is the time frame to do this after the disability or death of your partner?

Review your investment accounts, credit cards, bank accounts and credit lines? Do you have any of these titled together? Are you a joint holder, or a single user? What will be your limits on future access to cash assets? What is your possible financial liability for the balances owed?

If you really want to protect your partner and children, if it applies, you need to take responsible action now. But how? With the help of a team consisting of a qualified attorney and a qualified financial professional to design and assist you in implementing a complete package for your non-traditional family Then you need to periodically update your plans as your situation changes. Any issue that is not addressed in a valid legal document is an issue that is in jeopardy of physically, emotionally and financially harming your partner at the time of your death or disability.

Time to Get Started

On the next page, you'll find a chart/case study for a non-smoking, self-employed family with a 43-year-old male, his 39-year-old wife and their two children, a "typical" family of four with a $5,500 HSA deductible plan in place.

You can see how the cost and benefit arrangement of the typical family spending their $14,500 on only premiums and out-of-pocket costs pales in comparison to the case study scenario with the same type of health care needs. Are you hesitating for financial reasons? The worst excuse has to be "I can't afford it." This confirms you are closer to the edge of financial disaster from a medical cause than you may be willing to admit.

Monthly policy premiums on HSA Plan that includes optional prescription coverage. 100% deductible if you are self employed.	$370.67 x 12	$ 4,448
30% estimated Tax savings as a self-employed person on premiums		-1,334
Annual Family Deductible (Money deposited and not used in this plan year can be left to accumulate tax-free for expenses in future years, or for medical expenses after retirement)		5,500
Co-pays after deductible 0%		00
30% estimated tax savings on HSA contribution		-1650
Combination policy including: $100,000 lump-sum catastrophic illness policy on Husband, $100,000 lump-sum catastrophic illness policy on Wife, Plus a $10,000 rider for each child		1,803
$4,600 a month private disability policy on husband with a 90-day elimination period with benefits payable to age 65. Includes optional return of premium rider. If the benefit is never used, at age 65, this insured would receive back $30,800 or about 89% of premiums paid over the life of the policy. In the event some benefits were used, the premium refund would be less.		1,573
$4,600 a month private disability policy on wife with a 90-day elimination period with benefits payable to age 65. Includes optional return of premium rider. If the benefit is never used, at age 65, this insured would receive back $55,191 or 100% of premiums paid over the life of the policy. In the event some benefits were used, the premium refund would be less.		2,123
Minimum medical exposure is premiums only		9,947
Maximum medical exposure with full deductible utilized for medical care, less estimated HSA tax savings for a self-employed family		12,463
RESULTS		
Maximum medical exposure with full deductible utilized for medical care, less estimated tax savings for a W-2 family		$13,797
National average for a family of four For premiums, co-pays and deductibles only		$14,500

STOP & THINK

You could be poised to lose everything in a short period of time because of procrastination or denial. Perhaps you are concerned about the time and energy it will take you and others to implement changes. Or are you not ready to face the inevitable fact that you may become disabled, and/or not recover from a disability? Yes, it can be frightening to consider the scenarios, but with support from family and friends you can all get through it without financial devastation. Just remember, you and your family have everything to lose by not doing anything at all now that you know what to do.

Amy Rose Herrick
4536 SE 37th Street
Topeka, KS 66605
785.379.0586 (tel)
amy@amyroseherrick.com
www.amyroseherrick.com

Amy Rose Herrick, ChFC, IAR has been involved in the financial industry for most of her working life. Amy assisted a nationwide base of institutional investors with portfolio management from 1985-1990. In 1991 she changed the focus of her consulting services to devote her years of financial expertise and skills exclusively to individuals; specializing in the multi-faceted needs of small business owners.

Amy develops highly personalized Comprehensive Financial Plans. Each plan is developed on a case-by-case basis, which focus on the specific financial situation of the individual or business. Clients are provided with a written plan that coordinates company benefits, pro-active income tax reduction strategies, debt structuring, cash flow analysis, personal insurance, and portfolio management including structured investment and also distribution and estate planning.

Amy has served in the local community in numerous capacities, contributing heavily to charity and serving on non-profit boards. Typically, her involvement evolves into serving in an officer position. Amy continues to share and grow her financial knowledge with the public as a published author and financial columnist, and maintains on-going education and professional licensing to practice in several states. She has spoken at numerous events and is available for media interviews.

5. Retirement Planning

Larry V. Parman, JD, RFC, CFWC
Parman Financial Advisors, LLC

The purpose of this chapter is not to provide specific advice about how to invest your money during retirement years. Nor is it to remind you that all investments have risk — which they do — or that no one can appropriately guarantee you a specific investment return — which they cannot. Rather, it is to share a new perspective about your retirement finances, help you develop a process for approaching this vital subject, and show you a process that can help to improve your financial security during this most important time in your life.

Let's start by asking, "Why is retirement planning this important?" The first answer is simple: You're going to live longer than any previous generation in the history of this country. And for most of us, there is a widening gap between our retirement age and our life expectancy. In the United States we still retire around 65, but many of us will live into our mid-80s. Our retirement funds have to work harder and last longer, or we run out of money before we run out of time. And that does not even take into account a financial legacy we may want to leave our heirs.

In the upcoming pages we will share new perspectives about retirement planning to help you create a more effective retirement plan and, hopefully, enjoy your retirement years even more.

Seek Professional Help

First, seek excellent professional help. Yes, I'm a financial advisor. Yes, it serves my interest to say and believe this. It also serves yours, but for reasons other than you may think. You may be used to doing your own financial planning or wealth management. You might even think you're a pretty good investment manager. You have access to information. You have the time. You have the interest. You're as smart — or smarter than — your advisor. You say, "Look at what I've done in the past five years!" Bravo. During that period, everyone did well. You may not need a professional advisor to help you with the mechanics, analysis or decision-making concerning your investments. You need one to help you to design a realistic plan. You need one to separate reality from fantasy and keep them separated during your retirement years. Nothing could be more harmful to your retirement years than thinking you're an investment genius rather than a passenger on a boat being lifted by a rising tide. A good advisor will not eliminate the downside. He or she will minimize its impact and help you follow a very good rule — do no damage.

> Nothing could be more harmful to your retirement years than thinking you're an investment genius rather than a passenger on a boat being lifted by a rising tide.

If you choose a professional advisor, I suggest you work with a registered investment advisor (RIA). RIAs have a *fiduciary duty* to you. That means they have to satisfy a court of law that what they recommend is in your best interest. The typical broker has a *suitability standard* to you. Sure, you want recommendations to be suitable. But if it were me, I'd want the higher requirement. It doesn't confer competence on anyone, nor does this mean your broker is unable to help you. Think of it as an insurance policy. When you're planning for your retirement it's a premium I recommend you pay.

Your Retirement Begins at Age 5!

You think retirement begins at 65 or at some age when working every day is no longer part of your life. You're wrong. It begins around age 5! Think about it. Isn't that when it begins? Our behavior and attitude about money form at a very young age. Here's the best example: At a very early age your parents bought you something simply because Johnny next door had one.

Or because someone — Dr. Spock, Oprah, or another accepted media guru — said you couldn't be a normal kid without one. From those early experiences correlations were made, behaviors were influenced, reinforcement took place. Outcomes 50 years down the road were determined. And what's more, we grow to think our experience is "normal," thereby making changes in our attitude about money very difficult.

> *You should think of investing for retirement as a life-long process that begins early in your life.*

But you're not 25. You're 35, 45, 55, 65 or older. Now what do you do?

A Retirement Planning Process That Works

When retirement planning, many financial advisors make the mistake of focusing only on your investments. That's a big mistake. You want your retirement planner to treat you like your doctor treats you. Think about it: If you went to a doctor with a pain in your arm the doctor would likely look at your arm. She would also look at other parts of your body, because it's possible that your heart, for example, could be the cause for the pain in your arm. Just as the various parts of your body work together, so do your finances. That is why it is essential that if you are going to truly address your overall financial needs, you must review all of the essential parts of your financial picture. I refer to this as a full financial check-up that addresses all of your financial needs. Such a check-up consists of reviewing five critical areas of your financial life: protection issues, estate planning, income tax matters, retirement planning and investment management.

Although each of these areas is dealt with separately, they are really all interconnected. If you reduce your taxes, this will allow you to invest more, which in turn will help you retire earlier or live more comfortably during your retirement years. If you need more income from your IRA, you may have to pay more income taxes and this could change the investment mix inside your portfolio. Another way to look at it is that if you invest properly, you can reduce your taxes, which, again, will help your income during retirement. However, if you do not hold title to your investments properly, you may need additional insurance for protection against estate taxes. The last three areas — income tax, retirement planning and investment strategies — usually require the most time, and are usually the areas of highest interest.

STOP & THINK

You might want to have copies of your brokerage accounts, estate planning documents, income tax return, estimated monthly expenses, insurance policies and financial goals in front of you so we can look at each of these areas. Because some of the topics are covered elsewhere in this book, we will focus on income tax, investment and retirement planning in detail.

Protection Issues

It is important to touch on all areas of insurance coverage, including your homeowners, automobile, umbrella, medical and life insurance. Failure to review them can cause a major liability problem down the road. There may be special opportunities with existing life insurance policies that deserve special attention. At a minimum, if you decide you need continued life insurance, you should have the policy audited for performance. Many older policies have no guarantee in their coverage. This means that as you get older the mortality cost will deplete your cash value and the policy will terminate before you do. One day you'll get a call telling you that if you want to keep the policy in force you'll have to pay annual premiums far in excess of what you've been paying. If you have that exposure, you need to know it now.

Long-term health care insurance deserves special attention because it is becoming a critical component of your retirement plan. It's also an area that meets at the intersection of financial and estate planning. You should have your financial and legal advisors work on this issue together. If you are in an excellent financial position, you should be able to afford making the payments to an at-home caregiver or a nursing home. However, it's frightening to think of spending $4,000–$5,000 a month. At that rate it doesn't take long to deplete your estate. Many of you are concerned about this issue, so you should review your options with your financial advisor and estate planning attorney.

Estate Planning

The next area, estate planning, is likewise fundamental. This is an area where procrastination seems to prevail. We keep putting it off. Who wants to discuss death and taxes? Your advisor will ask you questions to determine what planning has been completed; for example, whether you have a living trust, along with all of the other documents such as durable powers of attorney, community property agreement, health care documents and so forth. This individual may recommend a review and update of your estate plan, either with your attorney or one they recommend.

Make sure you have your estate plan reviewed at least once every three years, and please have it reviewed immediately in the event that you or your spouse are not in good heath!

As part of this process, you should review your investments to determine the beneficiary of the IRAs and how you hold title to your other assets. If you have a trust, it's been estimated that less than 50% of the assets are titled properly in the name of the trust; thus failing the "avoid probate" test. This should be thoroughly explored.

As you review beneficiary designations, you should consider whether you are interested in the possibility of stretching out your retirement accounts over the next 50, 60 or even 70 years so that your heirs will not have to pay income tax on the distributions immediately after you pass away. Be aware, this is another area in which some advisors have little knowledge or expertise.

Income Tax Planning

I've never met anyone who did not want to reduce their taxes. A study from the Boston-based financial research firm Dalbar, Inc. shows that most investment professionals are out of touch with their client's need for tax information. Out of more than 4000 individual households polled, more than 80% of the respondents wanted to receive investment-related tax information from their financial advisors, but usually were not receiving such information.

If your investment advisor doesn't know how to read and understand your tax return, you need another advisor. How can they make an investment recommendation without knowledge of tax brackets, alternative minimum tax, and so forth? You want to work with an advisor who will assist you with tax planning even though another professional may prepare the return. Any money they help you save on taxes is money that will flow right back into your pocketbook.

Retirement Planning

Your advisor should gather information about your retirement plan by actually reading your plan agreement. This is, obviously, the only way the advisor can give adequate advice about your options. One of the main issues with a company retirement plan (pension, profit sharing, 401(k) or other retirement plan) is to get a distribution request form and make sure that you and the advisor have enough information to do a direct transfer into an IRA.

STOP & THINK

This will also allow your advisor to prepare a report showing the tax consequences of 10-year averaging versus ordinary income versus rolling it over into an IRA. This is a simple yet effective way to illustrate why you will want do an IRA transfer rather than paying the taxes.

We also have to determine what some today refer to as "The Number."[1] How much will you need each month during your retirement years? Here's what I've learned: It's more than you think, and rules of thumb are almost worthless. I've also learned that behavior is almost as important in determining how much you need as the return you'll earn on your portfolio. That said, how do you approach this?

Calculate your expenses. I know, you're thinking, "Is he telling me to create a budget?" Yes, a reality budget, not a fantasy budget. Cash flow is an important issue for anyone facing retirement, yet many people don't keep very good records of their actual expenses. Because this is a key factor in making retirement decisions, if you don't know how much you are spending, you should keep a budget or fill out a cash flow analysis for monthly expenses. Until you can tell your advisor "The Number" — the amount you'll spend each month — it's nearly impossible to create a relevant plan.

So have an honest discussion with yourself about after-tax cash flow. Again, to determine "The Number," it's important to deal in reality rather than fantasy. You can only spend after-tax cash flow. If you do not have enough money coming in to make ends meet, your financial plan is not going to work. If you are spending your principal now in order to get by, it is only going to get worse in the future. Be sure to call it the way it is. If you are retiring at a young age, such as 55, then you'll have 15 more years of uncertainty than someone who retires at age 70. If you're spending most of your income and all of your investment savings early on in life a good advisor will frankly point out the implications. If they won't, they are not the advisor you need. It will only get worse in the future due to inflation or other uncertainties. Deal in reality, not fantasy.

The Critical Role of Investments in Your Retirement Years

This is a major area most advisors usually address first, when they should address it last. After you know "The Number," you're ready to discuss how your portfolio can help generate it. You should first have a conversation about a

---

[1] "The Number: What Do You Need for the Rest of Your Life and What Will It Cost?" by Lee Eisenberg

number of basic concepts that impact your investment outcomes.

Start by asking your advisor to explain how risk impacts your portfolio. Years ago, my first boss told me, "Risk is commensurate with yield." It's still true. One dramatic difference between the amateur investor and professional advisor is that the investor will be thinking of return and the advisor will focus first on risk. Reducing risk should be an important factor in your investment selections. All securities and mutual funds have quantitative measures of risk. Have your advisor explain how "beta" works and show you the different betas between your investments and their investments. Having an advisor say, "I do not want to get you the highest return on your investments; I am interested in achieving the highest return with the least amount of risk" is sweet music to your ears. Most of us appreciate the fact that an advisor would rather utilize safer techniques to help us achieve our goals.

Learn about a concept called "sequencing of returns." In most cases, you're better off to exchange risk for consistency. This is one of the most challenging areas of investing because we read the headlines about returns that are higher than those of our own portfolio and we start doing stupid things. We get emotional. We chase returns. That's a huge mistake and one you should avoid at all costs if you have any hope of long-term portfolio success. Below is a simple example of the value of consistency and impact of sequencing in investment returns.

If you invested $10,000 for each of the next five years and the investment returns were:

Year 1: 10%

Year 2: 10%

Year 3: -20%

Year 4: 10%

Year 5: 10%

At the end of year five, your portfolio value would be $11,713.

On the other hand, if you invested the same $10,000 and the returns were 7% in each of the five years your portfolio value would exceed $14,000.[2]

---

[2] This is a hypothetical example used for illustrative purposes only, and does not represent the return of any specific investment. Actual rates of return will vary over time, particularly for long-term investments.

STOP & THINK

Focus on total return over yield. It is important to take a moment to understand this idea. Many times we can only relate to the income generated, not the actual appreciation/total return. For example, if you want an 8% return on your money and you need a monthly check from this source, it is imperative that you understand that a 30-year treasury bond is now only 6%, and it is getting more and more difficult to generate dividends greater than 7% from equity investments.[3]

As we mentioned earlier, you have to factor in taxes and inflation when planning for your retirement. Failure to do so will leave you very disappointed in a few years. Before you retire, growth investments are probably more appropriate. However, after retirement, you may have more of a need for income rather than growth.

Now we're ready to discuss the portfolio. How should you approach the investment portfolio during retirement years?

You need to determine how much you need to keep in your reserve account. You should have enough money to cover six months to one year of required income (less Social Security and guaranteed pension income) and handle significant upcoming expenditures. This means taking into account how much you might need for an upcoming trip, a new kitchen, roof repairs, a new car and so forth.

In addition, you want enough left in the bank to put you on what I refer to as "safe ground." There's an amount of money you like having in the bank that gives you peace of mind and comfort. For some it might be enough to cover your cash flow requirements for one year, over and above Social Security and other guaranteed income sources. For others, it might be less. Nonetheless, all of us have a safe ground number.

Now we know about how much is available to invest. At some point diversification will enter the conversation. How many times have you been reminded to diversify your portfolio? What's less clear is how to do it. Most of us think diversification means buying a bundle of different stocks or mutual funds. In fact, many times prospective clients come in for a financial review and tell us they're diversified. Our portfolio review confirms they do in fact have different stocks or funds. But, they're all large-cap U.S. stocks or funds. That's not diversification. This is where expert financial advice is worth the money. Even if you feel the market is going to go up or go down, you could

---
[3] *Wall Street Journal*

still be wrong. Remember Murphy's Law: If something can go wrong, it will, and at the worst possible time! Instead, you should explore multiple investment strategies, including asset allocation, with your advisor.

> *The benefit of asset allocation is that something usually doesn't go wrong with everything at the same time.*

Here's what you should know about this very important concept.[4]

What is Asset Allocation?

Asset allocation is a disciplined strategy of investing in several asset classes, such as stocks, bonds, cash, real estate, energy, and so forth. In other words, you do not put all of your eggs in one basket. In an asset allocation strategy the most important decision an investor makes is what percentage of the portfolio to allocate among different asset classes.

For example, as a moderate investor you might allocate 50% of your portfolio to a variety of equities, 40% to fixed income, 5% to energy and 5% to real estate. As you get a little older you might become more conservative and reduce your equities allocation to 35-40%. Any of these percentages can be changed based on circumstances and need.

At each stage in the investment planning process you will have to carefully examine your investment time

"Laddering" to Minimize Risk

For the fixed income portion of your account the advisor might mention the concept of "laddering." This is a strategy to help minimize exposure to interest rate fluctuations. Instead of buying CDs or bonds that are scheduled to come due during the same year, you would purchase CDs or bonds that mature at staggered future dates. For example, you invest $20,000 each in a one-year, two-year, and three-year CD or bond paying 5%, 5.25%, and 5.5% respectively. At the end of the first year, you reinvest the proceeds from your 5% CD or bond and buy a 5.5% CD or bond maturing in three years. Because you are able to reinvest a portion of your money each year, you are less exposed to interest rate fluctuations.

---

[4] Diversification of your overall investment portfolio does not assure a profit or protect against a loss in declining markets.

horizon and risk tolerance. For those who are younger and have a longer time horizon and high-risk tolerance, a portfolio with a higher percentage of risky assets, such as stocks equities, might be more appropriate. That said, be careful here. You might think you are being brave by answering questions from a risk tolerance survey one way only to discover your stomach can't tolerate the market volatility your ego thought it could. Sometimes experienced investment advisors recognize this attitude in investors. It shows up as "I know more than you do and I can outsmart the market." Good luck.

Be realistic in your expectations, in your understanding of the history of the market, about your risks, about your goals and about how much you want to sleep at night. If you make a major mistake during retirement years, you may not have enough time to recover your losses and avoid running out of money.

It's important to note that every asset has risks. For example, an FDIC-insured CD exposes investors to the risk of the investment not keeping up with the rising price levels of goods and services. This is more commonly known as inflation risk. Other asset classes have historically outperformed CDs. They have a higher expected return, which compensates investors for taking more risk. This risk premium explains why investors are willing to invest in riskier assets.[5]

In addition to the type of assets you should own through multi-asset class diversification, a professional financial advisor will educate you about style and management diversification of your investment selections.

Portfolio risk can also be reduced by investing in assets that do not rise and fall in value at the same time. "You mean that while some of my assets are increasing in value I want others to decline?" Yes. In fact, it's ideal when one asset falls in value at the same time the other rises in value. This situation can dramatically reduce the overall volatility of your portfolio, because the two assets offset each other. The lower correlation between assets in the portfolio results in lower overall portfolio volatility and, therefore, risk.

---

[5] CDs are federally insured up to $100,000 per deposit, per institution. Offer a fixed rate of return, and are subject to change and availability.

There are many key benefits to multi-class investing. Asset allocation helps take emotion out of the investment management process. It helps reduce the risk of poor return sequencing as we previously discussed. Some call it the "ugly math" problem of portfolio losses. If an investor loses 20% of the portfolio value in one year, it takes a 25% gain the next year to break even. If an investor loses 50% in one year, then it will take a 100% return in the following year to break even. More moderate losses in down years — yes, Alice, there will be down years — minimize the "ugly math" problem. Finally, asset allocation helps reduce risk and portfolio volatility. Lower volatility allows money to compound at a faster rate.

There have been numerous studies on the merits of multi-asset class investing. A study published by Roger Ibbotson and Paul Kaplan in the January/February 2000 issue of *Financial Analyst Journal*[6] concluded the percentage of variability of returns across time explained by asset allocation policy equaled 90%. In other words if Portfolio A returns 12% and Portfolio B returns 9%, asset allocation differences are typically responsible for 2.7% (90% of 2%) of this difference. Only 0.3% (10% of 3%) of this difference is attributed to other factors.

A study by Gary P. Brinson, Brian D. Singer and Gilbert L. Beebower reported in the May/June 1991 edition of the *Financial Analyst Journal*[7] determined that the asset allocation of a portfolio explained 93.6% of the variation in its total returns. It concluded that individual security selection was a rather insignificant determination of the change in portfolio value.

A study by Gary P. Brinson, Brian D. Singer and Gilbert L. Beebower reported in the May/June, 1991 edition of the *Financial Analyst Journal*[7] determined that the asset allocation of a portfolio explained 93.6% of the variation in its total returns. It concluded that individual security selection was a rather insignificant determination of the change in portfolio value. Other studies confirm the risk-reducing power of asset allocation. It's one strategy you should learn more about.

Now you have your plan in place. The next decision is how much you can take from your portfolio to fund your living expenses?

[6] *Financial Analysts Journal;* http://www.cfapubs.org
[7] Ibid

STOP & THINK

What's a Withdrawal Rate and Why Does it Matter?

Investment returns are very important in creating a secure retirement. Equally important are the withdrawal rates on investment capital to meet personal living expense requirements. Cash flows vary from year to year. We must consider all sources of income. Some — Social Security for one — will be adjusted for inflation. Some — fixed pension payments, for example — will not. The impact of variable cash flows will greatly affect the extent you need to dip into the principal of your retirement portfolio.

The goal is to not outlive your money. Said another way, you don't want to deplete your portfolio during your lifetime. Let's review a few guidelines about how much you can safely withdraw from your portfolio.

> Naturally, your portfolio should be designed to reflect your goals. But, it should not be asked to do more than it's capable of doing. This is a big challenge with some investors.

If you're going to depend on your retirement funds for 30 years and you're a conservative to moderate investor, some research suggests your retirement fund should be about 25 times larger than your first year withdrawal. That suggests a withdrawal rate of 4% in the first year. If you're willing to allocate a larger portion of your portfolio to equities, there's a good chance you'll have a significant balance at death. Of course, doing this will subject you to more risk, variability and volatility of annual returns.

Naturally, your portfolio should be designed to reflect your goals. But it should not be asked to do more than it's capable of doing. This is a big challenge with some investors. Once you know "The Number," your advisor can design a strategy to meet that requirement. There's always a tug of war between what's needed and what can be expected, given your risk profile. A Monte Carlo[8] financial probability analysis suggests that if you withdraw 4% each from your investments there's a 90% chance that your portfolio should last 30 years. The reciprocal suggestion is that if you need $50,000 each year you'll need a portfolio of $1.25 million in it to be 90% sure you won't run out of money. And, that's pre-tax. That's a reality check for some of you.

Once your plan is designed and implemented, review it quarterly. If you

---

[8] IMPORTANT: The projections or other information generated by the Monte Carlo Theory regarding the likelihood of various investment outcomes are hypothetical in nature, do not reflect actual investment results, and are not guarantees of future results.

have an asset allocation strategy in place, your advisor will want to re-balance the various asset classes from time to time. Let the plan work and do its job. You've gone about it the right way. You don't need to look at the ticker tape every day. Your quarterly reviews are a good time to re-evaluate performance and goals and make necessary adjustments. As you go through this process there will other factors that will influence your investment performance.

Behavioral Finance and Other Non-Financial Factors That Impact Investment Success

Human psychology may have more impact on your investment returns than the performance of your security or fund selections. That's because our risk and return perceptions often trigger emotions of fear and greed. Those emotions cloud our judgment, impact our investment selections and affect our investment outcomes. A growing field called Behavioral Finance alerts us to the non-financial factors involved in this uncertain process. Recognizing that these factors are at work will help you become a better investor. Again, be realistic about the presence of emotions in the investment process. You are not immune.

Do you remember the 1987 movie *Wall Street* where Gordon Gekko stands up at a shareholder meeting and says, "Ladies and gentlemen, …greed, for lack of a better word, is good"? Do you remember the late 1990s, when tech stocks were the rage? Do you remember the scores of investors who let their greed trump common sense by investing a large portion, if not all, of their portfolio in hi-tech stocks? Do you remember hearing how they felt in 2001? Do you remember how long it took their portfolios to get back to break-even? Greed might have been good for Gordon Gekko. But it's bad for most investors, especially during retirement years.

Then there is optimism. In trying to find an edge or advantage in our investment selections most of us tend to give too much weight to information signals that support chasing high returns, and too little weight to their probability of success. In effect, investments perceived as having high-return potential tend to be overvalued. That's another mistake.

Do not chase returns you read others are receiving. And don't pick an investment for what it's done in the past. We have an amazing color-coded chart in our office showing how different asset classes perform quarter to quarter over the past five years. The performance of most sectors often vary significantly from quarter to quarter. You might re-read the asset allocation section of this chapter.

> *A good rule to remember is that past performance does not indicate or guarantee future performance.*

Choose wisely based on your strategy; don't chase history. It's a formula for failure.

Here's another behavioral factor: We tend to overreact and correlate future earnings growth of a company with past earnings growth. We look at historical numbers and end up buying those securities that had the higher price/earnings ratios. Yet studies tell us the lower price/earnings companies tend to perform better over time. And, of course, all of us tend to under-react to new information, especially when it is contrary to our own strongly held beliefs.

Because of these factors, some people cannot be successful investors—they meddle, they watch every tick in the market, they panic at the newspaper headlines, they say recognition of this reality is phooey, they are reactive, not proactive, they have no strategy. You can't make 15% in an 8% market and you can't achieve high returns as a conservative investor. Nor, if you're an aggressive investor, can you sleep like a baby like your friend who is a conservative investor?

There are more, but these give you a feel for the impact of emotion in investment choices. Take responsibility for your investment choices. A great advisor who understands investment concepts and the behavioral factors will be worth every cent you pay them.

Summary

What you want to achieve during your retirement is certain. You want to maintain your lifestyle and enjoy those things you put off to this time of your life. Yet other than Social Security and a possible pension income, many uncertainties stand in your way of achieving your desired retirement outcome.

The recommendations to seek professional advice, reviewing the five key areas of your retirement life — protection issues, estate planning, income tax, retirement planning and investment strategies — provide you a roadmap that will take you safely through the very best time of your life.[9]

***

[9] Securities offered through 1ˢᵗ Global Capital Corp, Member NASD, SIPC. Investment Advisory Services offered through 1ˢᵗ Global Advisors, Inc. These opinions are based on our own observations and third-party research, and are not intended to predict or depict performance of any investment. These views are as of November 1, 2007, and are subject to change based on subsequent developments. Information is based on sources believed to be reliable; however, their accuracy or completeness cannot be guaranteed. These views should not be construed as a recommendation to buy or sell any securities. Past performance does not guarantee future results.

Larry V. Parman
Parman Financial Advisors, LLC
10740 Nall Avenue, Ste. 160
Overland Park, KS 66211
913.385.9400 (tel)
lparman@parmanlaw.com (email)
http://www.parmanlaw.com

Larry Parman is CEO of Parman Financial Advisors, a company offering law, financial services and tax planning services. This unique offering of services provides clients an opportunity to coordinate planning goals and maximize financial results. Larry is a member of the American Academy of Estate Planning Attorneys. He is also a member of the Oklahoma and Missouri Bar Associations, the American Bar Association, and the Oklahoma City Estate Planning Council.

A Native Missourian, Larry received his Juris Doctorate from the University of Missouri-Kansas City in 1974. He is an Accredited Estate Planner with the National Association of Estate Planners and Councils and is licensed to practice before the U. S. Supreme Court. Larry is a Certified Family Wealth Counselor and a Registered Financial Consultant.

Larry has been active in community and civic organizations throughout his career. He served on the Board of Managers of CompSource Oklahoma, the State's worker's compensation insuance company, serving a two-year term as chair. In addition, Larry was a member of the Board of Oklahoma City's Junior Achievement Chapter for nearly 20 years, serving two terms as President. He and his wife, Darlene, have two adult children, Ali and Scott.

6. Optimizing Your Wealth: It's Not Just About the Money

Janet Ramsey, CFP®
Premier Advisor Group

W hat is your definition of wealth? Is it your cash, securities, real estate, business, cars or jewelry? I have asked this question often, and most people will answer that their wealth goes beyond the financial dimension, and they list such things as health, family, friends, influence, social networks, and organizations and causes they care about. Jean is a 65-year-old recently divorced retiree, and she described her wealth to me as "all those things in my life that are truly satisfying and make me happy." She is in the minority of people I know who, when asked if they would have any regrets if they were to die tomorrow, said, "No, I really wouldn't do anything differently, nor do I have unfinished business." She still has many people, interests and activities in her life she cares about, but she does not feel the restlessness and yearning that many others have often shared with me in such statements and queries as, "I sometimes wonder if this is all there is to life. Isn't there something more than this for me?

We search for answers to questions such as these by traveling down some commonly trod paths, such as a quest for more power. Owning financial wealth and money is often considered to be one of the most potent forms of power and prestige in our society. The *Chicago Tribune* recently published an article by Anne D'Innocenzio with the headline, "Latest Luxury Items Raise the Bar, $700,000 pens, $40,000 purses becoming new standards for wealthy." She writes that sales for luxury items are rising dramatically, as are the prices, and 30% of all luxury goods are sold in the United States. She describes the buyers as searching for the "unique and different." She writes that "John Vogel, faculty director at Allwin Initiative for Corporate Citizenship at Dartmouth College's Tuck School of Business, said the growth of disparity between the wealthy and middle class doesn't bode well for society. If the ideal life is owning a pair of $1,000 shoes, that's 'a terrible ideal for young people.'"

Less than three weeks after that article ran in the *Chicago Tribune, The Wall Street Journal* published an article with the headline, "Giving Till It Hurts" by Sally Beatty. She writes that "nonprofits say they are receiving an increasing number of 'stretch' gifts, donations seemingly out of proportion to the givers' resources. To the shock or chagrin of friends and family, these gifts often require donors to make sacrifices or at least live more modestly than their income would allow." Beatty also writes, "Academics who study wealth say more aging Baby Boomers are choosing charity to add meaning to their lives — and to get a buzz that lasts longer than the kick that comes from splurging on a designer watch or expensive car."

> Those who seek more happiness and fulfillment in material goods, personal services and thrilling adventures, often find they need to keep "upping the ante" to continue experiencing gratification.

What disparate chosen paths! Those who seek more happiness and fulfillment in material goods, personal services and thrilling adventures, often find they need to keep "upping the ante" to continue experiencing gratification. While money may certainly prevent some unhappiness, happiness itself is not to be found in material wealth. There are many who feel that once essential lifestyle needs are met and if they refrain from comparing what they have to what others have, they are able to discover more meaningful and fulfilling paths to deeper satisfaction and to truly enjoying their wealth. Those who attain such a state in life arrive there through various paths and decisions that are appropriate and indeed must be appropriate, for their own unique situations.

Victor Frankl, psychiatrist, Holocaust survivor and author of *Man's Search for Meaning*, researched and wrote about his theory that our primary drive in life is not toward pleasure, but toward the discovery and pursuit of what we personally find meaningful. He argues that finding a purpose in life that is motivating to an individual can even solve many mental malaises and types of depression.

For many years, in advising clients and training advisors, I focused my advice primarily on the financial aspects of a client's wealth, as was the general and seemingly universal approach of the advisors who helped to train me. I was puzzled and sometimes frustrated when a client or family would not agree to take action and follow the advice their CPA, estate planning attorney and/or I gave them, often after a lot of work, analysis and thought went into how best to serve that client. When this occurred, I observed it wasn't due to bad advice being given. In fact, the advice was very good and appropriate in most cases.

If there was not a shortage of good advisors or advice, I asked, why wasn't the client taking this good advice? Then I realized that the advisor community is generally well versed in the financial aspects of wealth planning. However, the financial benefits alone are simply not motivating enough to move many to take concerted action and make changes in their plans. People need to have a motivating purpose they have discovered for themselves and be committed to that purpose to move ahead and make changes with confidence and clarity.

Life Stages in Wealth Planning

To discover our own motivating purpose and thereby create a satisfying rest of the journey and happy ending to the story of our lives, it is helpful to take a look at the overall path or life stages in wealth planning.

I. Financial Dependence — Three Phases

a. *Total Dependence* — This phase generally lasts from birth until your first job where you earn monetary compensation. You depend on resources from a separate source for your lifestyle and expenses. Some are born or marry into wealth and may never work for compensation during their lives. For them, this phase psychologically may last a lifetime.

b. *Partial Dependence* — You earn part of the financial support for yourself but still depend on some outside resources for the rest. Most two-income families are in this category, unless they save and invest an amount equal to or greater than either of their incomes. Many young adults and recent graduates are in this category as well, still receiving some support from parents or other family members.

c. *Working for Yourself* — You depend on your income from work but are independent from the income or assets of others. When you reach partial dependence or the working for yourself phase, most planning focuses on accumulation of assets for future goals, planning for the distribution of already accumulated assets, and replacing human economic value lost if death or disability occurs during this phase.

II. Financial and Time Independence

A good description of this phase is when you have attained the position of being able to purchase 100% of your time. You could also think of this as the point in time at which your accumulated wealth is sufficient to maintain your lifestyle for the rest of your life without requiring you to work and earn additional earned income.

Many accumulation plans have, and have had, significant gaps. Some have not allowed for unexpected events, such as market downturns early in retirement, divorce, or a major illness or accident. When these do occur, there is usually no opportunity for a do-over. The result is often a forced diminished lifestyle and/or a return to dependence upon other resources.

Of course, many people have never even formulated an accumulation plan, or they have one in their own mind that they don't want to share with anyone. In his book *The Number: What Do You Need for the Rest of Your Life and What Will It Cost?*, Lee Eisenberg refers to "a question that ought to burn for everyone over 30 … How much money do you need to secure the rest of your life?" In his research for the book, Eisenberg asked people what their number was and how they were progressing on reaching it. He describes the significant levels of discomfort some people had with this line of questioning. Our emotions about money and wealth and our inability to communicate with others about this subject can be real obstacles to being able to reach financial independence or to even realize when we have actually attained it.

Many accumulation plans have been successful, of course, and more people than ever before are finding themselves with surplus wealth and financial independence, above and beyond what they need for their lifestyle maintenance. Traditional financial planning has often focused on attaining this level of financial independence and has not gone much further in terms of analyzing what needs to happen once you have arrived there.

Today in America, there is a growing number of people who are essentially born into financial independence; the wealth in their families was accumulated before they were born. For many, this situation, which on the surface would seem to indicate good fortune, creates a psychological struggle with self-worth, purpose, suspicion of others' intentions, anxiety and ambivalence. They face different challenges in terms of determining how to spend their time and how to raise children with grounded and balanced attitudes towards their family wealth. Many are also fearful of taking risks or losing their status in terms of lowering their net worth.

Whether their clients' wealth is earned or inherited, more and more financial advisors are focusing on the design, implementation and monitoring of a customized lifestyle distribution plan for their clients' assets. Most inheritors, retirees or soon-to-be retirees want their assets to generate the right amount of lifestyle income, adjusted for inflation, while minimizing income taxes. They want their investments to be allocated appropriately to reflect their risk tolerance, and in such a manner that there is little likelihood of running out of money before they and their spouse die. In addition, they want to be sure they have enough to cover unforeseen emergencies and health care.

With longer life-spans and fewer guaranteed government or corporate income streams coming their way, not to mention the overall complexity involved, people are turning more and more to advisors for assistance with this aspect of their planning.

Especially when we reach mid-life and beyond, the conundrum of how best to integrate and balance all these factors for an optimal distribution plan often becomes the point where wealth planning encounters a real conflict. If your financial advisor or estate planning attorney advises you to address some tax or family issues regarding the transfer of your wealth at death or incapacity, your own demise may now seem to be a little more likely to occur than it did when your were in your 30s and 40s. Yet if your advisors make recommendations that you start making gifts to others while you are still living and/or that you start transferring some of your assets into trusts or LLCs or partnerships, there can be a sense that you will lose control or that you may not have enough later and would regret having made some of those choices.

If you are like many people, there seems there will always be time to address those issues later, because you think death is probably going to be well down the road. In many cases, it appears likely that there will be some assets leftover that children or grandchildren will inherit, even if there are some taxes that will have to be paid at that time. At this point in the process, many choose not to take recommended actions and instead put off any major decisions. They may choose to focus their energy and attention on a life perhaps filled with more leisure time, new grandchildren, and/or more new challenges and projects.

A Change in Priorities

For a growing number of us, as we reach our 50s and beyond, our thinking begins to shift about our life and its meaning. We begin to reflect on our past and reevaluate and think more about our own life's purpose. The fascination and intensity of running life's financial race or enjoying our financial fortune begins to morph into winning the life race. About reaching the goal of your number, Lee Eisenberg writes, "Do you know what you want to do with it?" He continues, "The second half of life is being reinvented as we live on for decades, forging new patterns of work and recreation."

> "...the second half of life is being reinvented as we live on for decades, forging new patterns of work and recreation."
>
> — Lee Eisenberg, Author of *The Number*

Many of us begin to look at our independent years as an opportunity to give back, to make a difference, to get involved, to build a school, to help provide clean water or job training or a medical clinic. We also begin to think about the relationships we wish were different or better or closer or not so broken. We start to think about our dreams and wonder if we still have time to fulfill them. We begin to focus on the aspects of our wealth beyond the financial dimension. It is in these personal and social dimensions of our wealth where we can find what truly motivates us.

Within the personal aspect of our wealth, we have dreams we want to experience for ourselves and our families. We also want to leave a trace of ourselves that will last beyond our life. We want to make a difference within the institutions and causes we care about. The late Ernest Becker, a Pulitzer Prize winner, explains in his book *The Denial of Death* that our greatest fear is "not so much extinction, but extinction with insignificance."

Exhibit I. Pyramid of Priorities

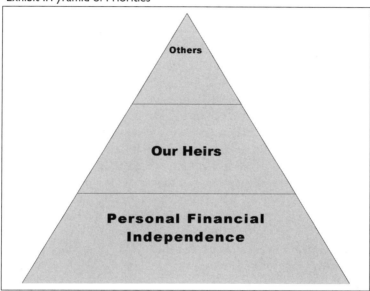

Exhibit II. Wealth Optimization

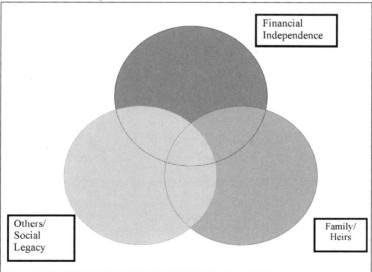

STOP & THINK

What if it were possible to use our financial wealth beyond meeting our own financial independence needs? It is in the skillful blending of financial, personal and social planning that we can 1) secure our own independence, 2) provide for our heirs and 3) make a difference by providing for the causes and institutions we care about.

For most people, there is a hierarchy of importance within these objectives, in just the order listed in Exhibit I, (page 81) but there is also an interrelationship (as depicted in Exhibit II, page 81). Most people would agree that a decision related to one of these objectives, for example, to spend more money on oneself, will have a negative impact on the other two areas. However, our tax code in the United States is written to allow the blending of these three goals by using tax-leveraging techniques in your wealth planning. In many situations, such planning can result in more income for you personally, an equal or greater amount to your heirs, and the ability to redirect tax dollars into substantial gifts to the charitable causes for which you care deeply. *In fact, often it is only through using charitable planning tools that all three of these can occur.* In the process, estate and capital gains taxes can often be eliminated or greatly reduced through carefully blended planning using all three dimensions.

Tom and Nora McLain[1] had three children and six grandchildren. They had done some traditional estate planning over the years and had wills leaving assets to each other, along with bypass trusts, health care and durable powers of attorney documents. Tom had started a plumbing business, which thrived over the years, and his son worked with him in the business. Tom and Nora were both involved in volunteer work with Habitat for Humanity and their church, and they liked the idea of planning using all three dimensions of their wealth. I told them I would begin a four-step planning process with them as follows:

1. Discovery: Getting Clarity About What You Want

2. Analysis: Evaluating What You Have

3. Design and Implementation: Deciding What You Need to Do

4. Monitoring and Maintenance: Have there been any changes since our last meeting?

In Exhibit III (page 83), the first three stages are depicted in the order and relative amount of time spent in each area. As time goes by, my clients and

---

1 Not their real names.

Exhibit III. Do/Have/Want

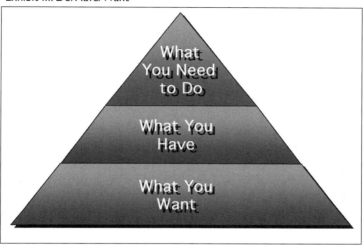

I review their plans, and the fourth stage of monitoring and maintenance begins the cycle anew, in a process of revisiting the first and second stages to determine if there have been changes in what they *want* or what they *have* and whether those will indicate additional things they need to *do* at that time.

I have seen some advisors and clients move too quickly to the top of this pyramid or the third step, "What You Need to Do," spending too little time or focus in the discovery phase or first step, "What You Want." By taking adequate time in this part of the process, I helped Tom and Nora clarify their values, concerns, fears, beliefs, agendas and dreams. I did this by asking questions and listening to their life stories, their early experiences with money and wealth, and their feelings about the future for their business, their children, their grandchildren and their community.

Although Tom was adamant that he really wanted his son to take over the business, Nora revealed that their son wanted to leave the family plumbing business and open his own landscaping business. This had caused conflict between Tom and Nora, as well as their son. During the discovery process, Tom and Nora learned about their own attitudes and behavior when making financial decisions and were able to quantify how much would make them feel financially independent in terms of lifestyle income.

Tom, Nora and I learned more about their family by talking about and exploring the unique differences in all three of their children. I asked, "Assuming there is surplus wealth, where do you want it to go?" When they replied, "To our children," I asked, "What is their degree of readiness and capability to manage a lump sum bequest at their parents' deaths?" Tom and Nora agreed that they wanted to more carefully transfer their wealth to their children, rather than making an outright bequest to each of them. We also discussed how they wanted to make a difference and be remembered. They shared how meaningful their charitable involvement was to each of them. They felt strongly that if taxes could be redirected to the charitable organizations they cared about, they would like to have that happen.

I summarized our discovery conversations in a written document, which captured their philosophy about their family, their mission in life, their values and their dreams. They shared this document with their children and other advisors. Their children expressed how thankful they were to be valued and trusted enough for their parents to share this information with them. They also were surprised about what they learned about their parents that they did not know before

We then moved to the analysis phase. When I did a diagnostic of their current situation, I found that if Nora died first, there was more than $1,500,000 that would go to federal and state estate and IRD taxes at Tom's subsequent death and that a little over $3,000,000 would go to their children. They were surprised at this news, as they thought they each could transfer $2,000,000 to heirs via their bypass trusts without any estate taxes incurred. The problem was that Nora did not own assets valued at anywhere close to $2,000,000 in her own name, as their assets were jointly owned or primarily in Tom's name. Tom and Nora wanted to rectify this situation, if possible. Using a cash flow projection tool, we were able to determine that their cash flow was more than sufficient to meet their lifestyle needs.

Tom owned one company stock currently valued at approximately $500,000. He had bought the stock many years ago for a $38,000 initial investment. He was reluctant to sell it, as he knew that would trigger capital gains. The stock was paying him about a 1.4% dividend. I recommended that he transfer that stock into a Gains Avoidance Trust (Charitable Remainder Trust). The trust could then sell the stock and would not owe any capital gains. The proceeds could be reinvested and generate a 6% rate of return for life for Tom and Nora. This increased their cash flow by $23,000 per year. Through this transfer, they also could receive an upfront income tax deduction of $85,000, which would shelter another $34,000 of taxes in their 40% combined state and federal income tax bracket. At the death of the second spouse, one-fourth of the remaining assets in the trust would go to Habitat and one-fourth to their church. The remaining one-half would go into a fund designated for future charitable gifting (a Donor Advised Fund), allowing their children to make ongoing distributions to charity. In addition to this money eventually funneling into their Donor Advised Fund, we also directed that any qualified plan assets from Tom's IRA that remained in the second spouse's estate go into this fund.

Tom owned the plumbing business and had a key employee who really wanted to take over the business when Tom was ready to leave. This made much more sense than forcing the business on their son, as Tom finally agreed. A buy-sell agreement was designed and executed and Tom was no longer concerned that this key employee would leave. An insurance policy owned and paid for by the employee guaranteed the value of the business to Nora or to the family should Tom die before the business transferred fully to the key employee.

We also recommended that Tom and Nora set up a family incentive trust into which their assets would funnel upon their deaths. This trust was designed to allow distributions to children and grandchildren under certain parameters for education, buying homes, medical expenses and starting businesses. It would be protected from bad decision-making, divorces, lawsuits and estate taxes for many decades following their deaths. They were able to transfer some of their excess cash flow into this trust now, allowing the trust to make current investments and insurance purchases. In addition, the value of the business and some other assets would go into the trust at the second parent's death.

Since we had determined that Tom and Nora's lifestyle income needs were protected for their lifetimes and their heirs would be taken care of, we were also able to determine that they could make some additional current gifts to charity right away and this really pleased Nora. She said, "I would so much rather enjoy seeing my gifts make a difference now while I am alive."

When we had designed this overall plan, with the help of their attorney and CPA, the end result was, assuming Tom and Nora lived to their life expectancy, their children and future generations would receive more than $4,200,000 through the Family Incentive Trust; charities (Habitat for Humanity, their church and their family Donor Advised Fund) would receive $3,000,000; and the IRS and state would receive $0.00. (See Exhibit IV, page 86)

STOP & THINK

Exhibit IV. Summary of Current and Revised Plan

Before Plan		Revised Plan to Life Expectancy	
Family	$ 3,108,180.00	Family	$ 4,240,000.00
Taxes	$ 1,540,000.00	Taxes	$ 0.00
Charity	$ 0.00	Charity	$ 3,000,000.00
		Increased Income/Yr.	$ 45,000.00

Tom and Nora expressed happiness and relief and said they were confident to go forward with my recommendations. They felt they understood more than ever before why they were making the decisions they were implementing and felt good about them. And I continue to monitor their situation, talk with them about what is important to them, and manage their plan to keep it on track and in congruence with their values and goals.

There are other helpful chapters in this book which go into more detail about gaining clarity around your goals (chapter 1) and finding the right advisor(s) to guide you in this process (chapter 10). The old paradigm of wealth planning was to have your advisors look only at the financial aspects of planning, almost immediately turning their attention to — and working on — recommendations of what you should *do*. The result was, and has often been, piece-meal, and not a very satisfying process.

The new paradigm of wealth planning is to integrate the financial, personal and social dimensions of your life into your planning by working with an advisor whose philosophy and skills allow them to facilitate this process for you. You will want this facilitating advisor to identify, include and communicate all of the above on your behalf to other appropriate specialists as needed, so that you have a team of coordinated and interacting professional advisors who all understand your personal story, your mission and your goals. This team will be able to provide different areas of specialized knowledge, viewpoints, and checks and balances against individual advisor bias, resulting in a more complete and creative game plan that better reflects what you want, your vision and your dreams.

If reading this has sparked an interest for you to do something differently in your own planning, I urge you to take action and find a specialist who can facilitate the overall process and help you get started now. Procrastination can be the greatest enemy when it comes to successfully maximizing the meaning and impact of your life's work, wealth, caring and wisdom. You may find it to be challenging, but the rewards and joy are worth it.

Janet Ramsey
Premier Advisor Group
3100 Tower Blvd., Ste 500
Durham, NC 27707
877.756.1805 or 919.475.3177 (tel)
jramsey@premieradvisorgroup.com
www.premieradvisorgroup.com

Janet Ramsey, CLU, ChFC, CFP®, is the founder and President of Premier Advisor Group, a founding partner of Galileo Group, and is a well-known financial educator, speaker and counselor to educational, nonprofit and professional groups throughout the nation. She has written and spoken on topics including Zero Estate Tax Planning, Tax Smart Strategies for Retirement Planning, Maximizing the Income and Estate Tax Opportunities with IRAs, and Family and Business Wealth Preservation.

For over two decades, Janet has assisted advisors and clients in creative ways to combine life planning with their financial planning to build legacies of significance based on personal values. Her counsel and assistance has resulted in substantial savings in estate and income taxes and greater retirement cash flow, and it has provided successful strategies for more meaningful multi-generational wealth preservation and family philanthropy.

Janet is currently a board member of the North Carolina Planned Giving Council. She also currently serves as Vice Chair on the Council of Alumni Affairs at the Kenan-Flagler School of Business at University of North Carolina-Chapel Hill. Janet is a member of the Financial Planning Association, the Advanced Association of Life Underwriters and Advisors in Philanthropy. She holds B.S., B.A. and M.B.A. degrees from the Kenan-Flagler Business School at the University of North Carolina-Chapel Hill.

Charitable Giving

Sally Alspaugh, CAP

Charitable giving reached a new record in 2006, an estimated $295.02 billion, according to the Giving USA foundation. The record-setting gift amount includes $1.9 billion that Warren Buffett paid in 2006 as the first installment on his 20-year pledge of more than $30 billion to four foundations and also includes donations from hundreds of millions of Americans, as well as gifts from charitable bequests, foundations and corporations.

What is surprising is that approximately 65 percent of households with incomes lower than $100,000 gave to charity last year. But, new IRS information about 2005 shows a very large change in giving by the wealthiest estates.[1] I offer you these statistics to make a point, not only that charitable giving is becoming increasingly popular among the average American, but it is also gaining in popularity among the most affluent individuals. The facts about the significant change in giving by the wealthy are encouraging because I find that most times I need to "give permission" to wealthy individuals to give some of their wealth away.

[1] Giving USA 2007, the yearbook of philanthropy published by Giving USA FoundationTM and researched and written by the Center on Philanthropy at Indiana University. For a copy of the report, www.givingusa.org.

STOP & THINK

More often than not, when I meet with wealthy prospects and clients in their 60s and 70s, they tell me stories of being raised on a shoestring, many living a life of frugality. It is surprising to many that in this stage of their lives, they have accumulated millions of dollars and yet they can't comprehend that they are indeed wealthy. As an example, I have worked with a very wealthy couple who found themselves in this situation, and needed help making gifts in the range of $50,000 rather than $500. They could very easily part with the larger sum but their experience was in making the smaller gifts. Their wealth was so large that they just couldn't comprehend their capacity.

Let me share a few more of my most memorable experiences with clients and their philanthropic events that added so much to their lives as well as the lives of others.

Case Study #1: Recent Widow Needs Permission

As an example, I had a meeting with a widow who needed my "permission" to go shopping for some new clothes and a new car. She was also considering buying a new house. In early 2006, she lost her husband and one of their two children within five weeks of each other, and was just beginning to emerge from her grief. She had no idea what to do to move her life ahead. Should she fix up some of the property that she and her husband owned? During our meeting, I explained that she had enough net worth and income to not only do what she was asking, but also to entertain some charitable giving. I suggested what I thought to be a most thoughtful gift to a nearby hospital for the enhancement of their breast imaging center to memorialize her daughter who died of breast cancer. "Oh," she said, "do you really think I could do that?" Not only did I think she could do it, I told her, for her own sake, she should do it. Tears came to her eyes and she thanked me profusely.

> Some individuals don't realize that they can get involved in causes and charitable giving on a personal level now, instead of waiting until they die.

Some individuals don't realize that they can get involved in causes and charitable giving on a personal level now, instead of waiting until they die. As example, a gentleman I met — a retired pharmacist — decided to leave his assets to his pharmacy school. I suggested and encouraged him to think about making gifts during his remaining years. I asked if he thought it would be a good experience to meet some of the pharmacy students that his scholarship money was going to benefit. He was surprised and asked me," You mean I could get to know some of those students now rather than waiting until I die and not meet them at all?" "Yes," I replied. It gave him an entirely new perspective on giving.

In his book, *Halftime: Changing Your Game Plan from Success to Significance*, Bob Buford's posture has greatly influenced me, and he explains how to make the *rest* of your life the *best* of your life. He recently asked me why the rich don't give more away. I pondered that question for a quite a while and came up with a few thoughts. One had to do with the emotional inclination toward scarcity instead of abundance. For instance, if you are afraid of losing your wealth it will be difficult for you to give some away especially if you believe you might need it someday.

Generosity more often flows when one has a sense of security about one's circumstances.

I don't believe I've ever met a generous person who was truly afraid of not having enough. The latter feeling, I think, completely overtakes the former and, instead, paralyzes the generous inclination. Haven't we all known generous people who don't have an abundance of wealth yet they are generous out of their own sense of well being and wanting to help?

In contrast, we all know some wealthy people unwilling to part with anything. Ironically, the individual with more than the non-taxable exemption in net worth, will end up parting with 50 cents of every dollar beyond the lifetime exemption in a very unceremonious and anonymous way at death through taxes. Their hard-won wealth that was earned, taxed, invested, and perhaps taxed again upon sale, will once again be taxed at death. This means that millions of dollars that could have been spent on philanthropic activities or on family members or friends will not. A thought-provoking question I ask individuals or couples of significant wealth is this: "If you gave away a million dollars to charity this afternoon, would you still be able to support your lifestyle?" Most say, "Of course, but no one has ever asked us that question that way before."

Case Study #2: The Million-Dollar Nun

Recently I met with a former nun who left her order after 23 years and then went to work for the next 19 years for a publicly traded company. She is now worth more than a million dollars but doesn't need a lot of money for her way of life. Her wealth accumulated as a result of a frugal lifestyle, some inheritance, and good money management. With no spouse or children as heirs, she named her five siblings, all in their 80s, in her will. I asked her if any of her siblings needed her wealth if she predeceased any one of them and she replied, "Probably not." Additionally, she mentioned she had 19 nieces and nephews and she knew that her brother's two children would inherit more per person than her sister's five children doing it the way she was planning. I suggested that she talk with her siblings and ask them if it would be okay to leave her assets directly to the next generation. That way each of the 19 nieces and nephews would inherit an equal amount. She said that she thought that would be all right with them, and she thanked me for the suggestion.

She also said she didn't need the required minimum distribution from her IRA and that last year she even gifted from her IRA directly to a charity. I told her that I was proud of her for doing that. Upon further thought, I quoted the current tax law that allows up to $100,000 to be transferred directly to a charity and told her that would take care of her minimum distribution for the current year. Although she gave only $5000 the previous year from her IRA, she said she would consider the $100,000.

Of course, the leap from $5,000 to $100,000 was significant, but in light of her net worth, I pointed out that instead of being worth $1.3 million she would now be worth $1.2 million. We both agreed that the difference was not so great when put in that context.

Case Study #3: "Obligation Gifting" Defeats the Cause

A client in his early 60s needed help in fulfilling his passion for the last quarter of his life. He wanted to be as generous as possible and to achieve as much personal fulfillment from doing so. He is worth between $10-15 million, and has already created a foundation. He and his wife have no children, yet his foundation has only $200,000 in it. I kept thinking, "What are you waiting for?" As I discovered, he was waiting for a guide to help him appropriately give his wealth away. He had been greatly affected by the loss of his father, and so I asked him how did he think he could best memorialize his father? I had touched a nerve because tears came to his eyes. I told him that he didn't have to answer immediately but that was his homework. After receiving his list of gifts for the past two years, we separated the causes he was passionate about from the ones he felt obligated to give to. We also segregated the "relationship" gifts. A relationship gift is the common practice of giving to charity because a friend asks you to. The reality is that the gift might not be made at all if the relationship was not the driving force. The goal is to discover what the last few years of a person's giving looks like. By doing so, I can point out that perhaps the "obligation gifting" has been satisfied and now more can be done to further the causes he is passionate about. Just how much is needed to say "thank you" for an obligation or gratitude type of gift anyway? Something to stop and think about.

> A relationship gift is the common practice of giving to charity because a friend asks you to.

Case Study #4: Establishing a Legacy — Children, the Great Outdoors and Education

A few years ago, I was asked to advise a couple in their late 80s who were worth $14 million. They had one son who had a family. The son knew that after both parents were gone he would inherit half that amount and the other half would go to the government. He understood that it would be better to leave some of that wealth in the community rather than paying taxes to the government.

We created a plan that allowed the son and his family to inherit approximately $12 million, the government would received $2 million, and charities would receive approximately $8 million. Now if that doesn't cause you to stop and think I don't know what else would. The gifting has already begun to the family as well as to charities. His father has since passed away and his mother in her 90s has given away plenty to charitable causes. And besides, she doesn't have to worry about her current income taxes due to the five-year carry-forward for her charitable deductions. As a result, she has been able to endow a chair for a local symphony, give a six-figure gift to her alma mater, and renovate a trailside museum for city children because she is passionate about the outdoors and education. In fact, this was the last gift her husband was involved with. Until this time, they usually gave anonymously but I asked them to think about their three grandsons." Wouldn't you like your grandsons to show their children some day, that their grandparents gave the money to renovate this park museum?" When I made it a visual question, they both agreed to use their name on the building as a memorial.

STOP & THINK

Case Study #5: Breast Cancer Gift — Helping Heirs and Women Everywhere Through Family Philanthropy

A client and friend of mine in her mid- 60s was diagnosed with breast cancer. About the same time, I was helping a local hospital raise funds to expand their breast imaging center. I mentioned the campaign to my friend and asked if she might be interested in participating. She was interested and I encouraged her to offer a naming gift that was her largest ever. Previously, she had made gifts anonymously, but this time she wanted her name to be a part of the hospital's breast imaging center. She was thinking down the road in terms of her daughter and granddaughters perhaps needing special care for themselves some day.

As we were negotiating the gift, I asked the foundation if they ever used a gift agreement. They did and sent the form over to me. I was surprised that it was a half page with lots of blank spaces to be filled in. Thanks to some heads-up thinking from a mentor of mine we were able to secure the provisions that if the breast imaging center would ever move from the proposed building, my donor's name would *go with the center* and not simply remain on the building. Also if my donor's funds were not used for the intended purpose in a timely manner, say 18 months, she could redirect her gift, still within the foundation. These ideas gave the agreement some teeth and would protect my donor from being disillusioned both in the short and long run.

> Family philanthropy can be a powerful way to leave a legacy.

It was at a lovely dinner during which the announcement was made for the naming of the center and there were few dry eyes when she told her story. In attendance were friends of hers who were fellow breast cancer victims and survivors as well as the keynote speaker who, unbeknownst to everyone, mentioned that his first wife died of breast cancer about 30 years ago. It was a special and meaningful moment. Afterward, my donor friend/client said she felt like she was "coming out of the closet" as far as her charitable giving was concerned. She also mentioned that she thought her parents would be proud since it was through inheritance that she was able to make this gift. Thus, she acknowledged that four generations in her family will participate in the gift. Family philanthropy can be a powerful way to leave a legacy.

Case Study #6: When to Train Young People?

I met with a 35-year-old woman who was soon to receive access to her trust fund. She wanted to learn about managing money, so she gave me a call. Her father asked her why she was meeting with me and she said that he had been the one to encourage her to learn more about investments, yet clearly she did not have enough knowledge to manage her assets. Additionally, she had no real understanding of stocks vs. bonds and how various factors would influence her funds. So, she was old enough to have access to her accounts, but not to manage them intelligently. Sadly, Daddy was still doing that.

I believe in empowering young adults, even children, to be philanthropic in their lives, manage their own budget, and to acquire knowledge about money.

It's so important to teach the next generation to be wealth generators rather than wealth consumers. America won't be the same in the future if there are too many wealth consumers. Our country is great because of its wealth generators and innovators, including creative talent, not because of its consumers. One of my mentors told me that he believes teaching philanthropy is one of the best ways to teach young people about business and responsibility. These young people will one day have tremendous responsibility for themselves and others, so it is wise to help them at an early age.

Raising Financially Savvy Children: It's Time to Have That Talk

Often, I discover parents who are not gifting the annual exclusion amount to their children but, instead, are planning on dividing their estate among them through their estates. I ask them. "If you don't trust what your kids will do with the annual amount how can you trust them with a much larger amount? Start with the smaller amount and watch what they do with the money. Over time, I'm sure a pattern will develop." I ask them to watch and see if the annual amount is spent on fancy cars, for gambling, to pay off debt, given to charity, or invested. If a gift to charity is intended, do the children even know what charities are meaningful in the lives of their parents? Do the parents know what charities are meaningful in the lives of their children?

Here's where modeling and family storytelling becomes valuable. I have heard stories from 70-year-old clients who reminisce about their parents and the types of volunteer work they did, and the types of charities they helped. These clients often want to memorialize their parents by giving to those causes.

I have had meetings with my own family members who wanted to teach their children about generosity. They were now in a position to have a major gift fund established in their family's name through an inheritance. So the two teenaged children and their parents listed the names of the charities that they knew were important to them. Twenty-five names quickly emerged much to everyone's surprise. The parents instituted a program for their kids to gift $100 x their age on each birthday to as many significant charities as they wanted, but with the caveat that they wanted to see a six-month report on what the charity used the money for. That may help limit the number of charities they would give to, but it will also teach the concept of accountability.

A few years ago, I client of mine, gave a six- figure gift of gratitude to a university department. Recently, she wanted to give another large gift to the same cause only to discover that the original gift has yet to be spent for the cause for which it was intended. She was disappointed by this and decided to redirect her next gift elsewhere.

Too many times the important follow-up doesn't take place or the gift agreement wasn't negotiated in the first place and donors can become disillusioned with their giving. They ask, "Are my gifts actually doing what I intended? Since I don't hear from the charities, how do I know? Should I give more to a charity that I think is doing good but only communicates with me when they want more money?"

Unfortunately, many gifts, even from large accounts, end up being only "checkbook gifts" instead of meaningful and purposeful gifts.

I am hearing more often that donors are just not satisfied with their giving, and they feel there must be more to this.

While we are on the subject of younger children and giving, I once knew a grandfather who allowed each of his grandchildren to give $10 x their age to their favorite charity when they turned 10 years old. At his granddaughter's 11th birthday, he asked her, "Honey, are you going to give the gift this year to the same children's home that you gave it to last year?" "Oh no, grandpa,."

she replied." Why not?" he asked. His granddaughter said, "I found out that only 40 cents of every dollar actually goes to the children!" Can you imagine the stillness and the amazement from people in the room when I tell that story? Stop, do you think that the granddaughter will remember her grandfather differently than if he had just left her a trust fund of stocks and bonds? Wise grandparents know the answer.

Left Out of a Will? Annuity Payments from Charities

I Am Always Amazed

I interviewed a widow in her 80's who enjoyed entertaining each of her grandchildren during the summer at her lakeside cottage. She would ask each one what favorite dish she could prepare for them while they were visiting. One time a grandson asked for her famous sweet potato pie and her response was that he would have to wait until they returned to their home in the city because sweet potatoes were 10 cents a pound more at the cottage. This was from a woman worth millions! Perspective is often missing when one has lived a very frugal lifestyle or lived through the depression era.

Another female client of mine worried she wouldn't have enough to afford living in a nursing home if she needed to at some point in her life. I explained that she had enough wealth to *buy* a nursing home! She laughed and thanked me for my perspective.

Currently I am coaching a young widow who inherited much of her husband's wealth which included his business. She was feeling guilty because he left two older sisters out of the inheritance who are not so well off. I mentioned that my client could give money to her favorite charity for an annuity payment to the sisters that they couldn't outlive. She would get a current income tax deduction based on the ages of the sisters and her favorite charity would receive the remainder of the annuity after the sisters were deceased. The greatest appeal that this approach had was that she could be generous to the sisters but not put herself in the position of giving an outright gift whereby the sisters might spend the money and then be back for more. She asked me, rhetorically, what was wrong with the picture. We couldn't find much of a downside and now all parties are quite happy.

Who Are YOU Touching?

Think of fingerprints. Fingerprints left on a glass leave a tell-tale sign that you were using that glass. Your fingerprints will also remain on people, worthy causes, and on institutions — the ones you really care about. So, STOP AND THINK about this: What are the five most significant events in your life? How many of them have to do with money? I will venture to say that maybe one or, possibly, two may be among the most significant. But, the rest of your significant life events always have to do with the meaningful things you do for people. Think "philanthropy" and you will be rewarded in more ways that you can imagine.

Sally Alspaugh, CAP
11427 Reed Hartman Highway, Ste. 228
Cincinnati, OH 45241
513.618.6565 (tel)
sallya@sallyalspaughcap.com
www.sallyalspaughcap.com

Sally Alspaugh, CAP (Chartered Advisor in Philanthropy), is nationally recognized for her ability to bring clarity and common sense to the complex issues of income and estate tax avoidance.

An engaging educator, speaker and lecturer, Sally presents advanced strategies in layman's language interspersed with real life case studies and anecdotes. Serving as advisor to wealthy Cincinnati individuals and families for more than 30 years, Sally has conducted hundreds of presentations on topics that include Discovering Your Life Goals and Values, How to Legally Avoid Unnecessary Taxation, Transforming Taxable Capital into Social Capital, Building Family Legacies, and other approaches to family wealth planning for the affluent.

She has been a frequent guest expert for Cincinnati WVXU's "Law Talk" and WAXY 790 AM's "Funny Money" in Miami, Florida. For years, her column was featured in *Eastside Weekend's* financial section. Sally is a featured speaker for the International Association of Advisors in Philanthropy's monthly education teleconferences for industry professionals, and a contributing writer for *Thinking Beyond,* a quarterly client newsletter used by wealth advisors nationwide.

Sally is past president of the National Association of Philanthropic Planners and of Queen City Association, former Trustee of The Greater Cincinnati Planned Giving Council, member of International Association of Advisors in Philanthropy, former advisor to The Greater Cincinnati Foundation, and current advisor to The Bethesda Foundation. Among the organizations to which she has recently spoken are the United Way, Greater Cincinnati Foundation, City Ministries, Warren County Foundation, Jewish Federation of Cincinnati, University of Cincinnati Foundation, the Fine Arts Fund, St. Xavier High School and Xavier University. Sally holds a Bachelor of Arts degree from Denison University.

Sally and her husband, Jon, have one married son and reside on the east side of town with their two small dogs, Tigger and Winnie.

8. Legacy Planning

Mark Colgan, CFP®
Plan Your Legacy, LLC

All too often investors are solely focused on earning a high rate of return and minimizing the infamous tax bite. Minute by minute, Americans are informed about the current status of the financial markets and their investments through the various media. While this data can be interesting and occasionally helpful, it is also detrimental to our long-term vision. By focusing too much on short-term events, we develop tunnel vision and lose sight of the big picture — the purpose for growing our money. Although our society rewards people for making decisions based on intermediate ends, the best decisions in life are made with the ultimate end in mind.

Instead of focusing on how we are going to make our money grow, perhaps we should step back and ask ourselves why we want it to grow. In this sense, the "why" refers to the purpose behind your motive. It's great to gift $1 million to your children tax-free, but how is it going to influence their lives when they receive it? This deep-rooted question is a perfect example of how legacy planning goes beyond traditional estate planning. Legacy planning evokes introspective questions that are based on your values, not just your valuables.

STOP & THINK

Scott Fithian, one of the greatest visionaries of the financial services industry, dedicated the later years of his life to helping people better understand the true meaning of legacy.

> *"Legacy is heritage and heritage is tradition. Traditions are actions captured. Legacy is the most important tool any human possesses. The world will go on forever after we're gone. How will each of us positively impact its trajectory? That is legacy."* — Scott Fithian

Scott went on to say that when investors come to the realization that wealth is not measured in just dollars a whole new range of questions surface. What is the end? What is the larger purpose of my existence if not to win the game of accumulation? What is going to give my life meaning? Who am I as a person, and what is truly important to me? How have I made a difference and how can I make a difference in the future? What is the next mountain to climb? In essence, legacy planning is an opportunity to influence the well-being of your family, friends, and even the world beyond your own life.

Legacy Planning vs. Estate Planning

Legacy planning is clearly different from traditional estate planning. They both command an equal level of importance, but they serve different needs. Estate planning addresses your material possessions and legal affairs. Legacy planning, on the other hand, addresses your non-material possessions and personal affairs.

Interestingly, traces of legacy planning date back to the 15th century. Back then it was common for people to draft two wills, a legal will to handle the material possessions and an ethical will to document the family's values and religious beliefs. Together these documents provided survivors with invaluable information.

Today, legacy planning is re-emerging. In 2005, a landmark survey, The American Legacies Study[1], discovered that when defining a legacy, baby boomers and their parents feel that the non-financial things an individual

---

[1] Study commissioned by Allianz Life Insurance Company of North America (Allianz Life®), in conjunction with Dr. Ken Dychtwald, president of AgeWave.

leaves behind are 10 times more important to them than who gets the IRA or the stocks. Family members want to cover the really important issues, such as how someone wants to be remembered, the life lessons they learned, how their beloved pet is to be taken care of and who should receive their most personal belongings. In short, they're taking stock of their lives and looking for the clarity and control. Findings also showed that money wasn't high on the list. In fact, passing along "values and life lessons" was overwhelmingly considered (by more than 75%) the most important element of a legacy for both baby boomers and their parents' generation.

A Dichotomy Between Thought and Action

The American Legacies study also revealed that even though people felt legacy planning was important, many still weren't doing it. A similar study revealed the same irony. The Across Generations[2] study discovered that even the most prepared individual, who has a financial plan covering everything from newborn children to retirement, will often neglect to consider end-of-life details. In fact, unless you experience the death of a loved one firsthand, you may find it difficult to address such a sensitive issue.

It's important to understand why people prefer to discuss positive events over negative ones. It's human nature to want to discuss and look forward to significant life events, such as weddings, the birth of a child and retirement, because they create a sense of excitement and arouse a passion for life. Hence, people are naturally eager to talk about these milestones and want to plan ahead to ensure they are successful and memorable.

On the other hand, very few people are comfortable discussing the inevitable end of their lives, regardless of their age. Doing so requires that an individual face and confront their mortality — an understandably frightening prospect. As such, many of us ignore and avoid such thoughts and conversations at all costs. Because of this, most people rarely, if ever, discuss such plans until a personal crisis occurs in their life.

A Lesson from a Dying Man

It is said that part of living a good life is being prepared for its end. That's the lesson offered by Eugene O'Kelly, former CEO of accounting firm KPMG. In

---

[2] Across Generations Survey, MainStay division of New York Life Investment Management, LLC (www.nylilm.com)

STOP & THINK

May 2005, O'Kelly was diagnosed with terminal brain cancer. In the last four months of his life he wrote "Chasing Daylight: How My Forthcoming Death Transformed My Life," in which he urges everyone to spend time reflecting on their own mortality — before it's too late.

For those considering taking the time someday to plan their final weeks and months, O'Kelly has three words of advice: "Move it up." The legacy planning process allows you to plan your final weeks and months in advance, because as anyone who's experienced a sudden loss knows, death doesn't always give us fair warning. The fact is, with 2.4 million Americans dying each year — and that number continuing to grow — it is becoming more important than ever to have thoughtful, serious and personal conversations about life and death with your spouse and family.

So if you had four months to live,

- Would that motivate you to prepare for death?
- Would you take rudimentary steps to ensure your affairs were in order?
- Would you spend time reflecting on the values you learned in life?
- Would you attempt to communicate with your loved ones, making certain they knew of your love for them and how much you treasured your memories together?
- Would you make sure loved ones knew where to find important documents and information?
- Would you try, as best as possible, to reduce foreseeable disagreements over burial decisions or distribution of your belongings?
- Would you attempt in some small way to reduce the burdens on your grieving loved ones as you awaited the inevitable separation from them?

O'Kelly concludes by posing the question, "If how we die is one of the most important decisions we can make then why do most people abrogate this responsibility?"

Overcoming the Obstacles

All too often people postpone planning their legacy because they associate it with death rather than life. Additionally, we live in a world where the topic of death has become taboo, brushed under the carpet and never talked about. Some people are uncomfortable even thinking about death. To move forward, we need to change the way we view death. Instead of something to be feared, death can be viewed as a great motivator to do better, an opportunity to take life by both hands, to dismiss pettiness and live more fully each day.

Living life to the fullest actually helps us feel most prepared to die. As grief expert Elizabeth Kübler-Ross (1926-2004) explained: "It is those who have

A Lesson from a Survivor

Experiencing the death of someone you love is undoubtedly one of life's most difficult challenges. It is even harder if they die without a comprehensive legacy plan. The future you once had envisioned instantly disappears and your life is turned upside down. I know this all too well as I lost my late wife Joanne on 9/4/2001, just a week before the tragic events of 9/11. Our wonderful life ended abruptly and my life was suddenly changed forever. It went from fairytale bliss to tremendous, unbearable pain. I walked a path of introspection and carried on an internal debate about my purpose in life.

During this most difficult time, I also had to address all kinds of unwelcome, yet necessary, details. Within hours of her death I was writing her obituary, selecting her casket, planning the details surrounding her funeral, purchasing a gravesite for both of us and even designing her headstone. Within six hours I had gone from waking up with my wife to beginning the process of burying her. I also had to deal with a mountain of financial details that sprung up quickly.

Unfortunately these matters are not addressed in traditional planning. People typically consult with attorneys to create a will, healthcare proxy and/or power of attorney. They may even consult with a financial planner to better understand how to preserve their monies for future generations. But, typically, there are significant details that are often left unsaid, unplanned and open to guesswork after one's death.

Some might think that for a Certified Financial Planner™ professional like myself, such details would not be difficult. But like you, my emotions left little room for my normal logical and practical thinking. I remember asking myself, "If this is difficult for me, a certified financial planner, how does the average person even begin to deal with this?"

Joanne's will also left another void, one that was even more disconcerting. Joanne's memories, values and lessons that defined her life were never documented. Perhaps it was because her top-notch estate plan only focused on her material possessions and neglected to share what matters most.

not really lived — who have left issues unsettled, dreams unfulfilled, hopes shattered, and who have let the real things in life (loving and being loved by others, contributing in a positive way to other people's happiness and welfare) pass them by — who are most reluctant to die."

In many ways legacy planning is about life more than it is about death. And by going through the process of planning your legacy you can overcome your fears and live a more enjoyable and meaningful life.

Many people also avoid planning their legacy because they erroneously believe it might introduce conflict among family members. Studies have shown this fear is often unfounded. More significantly, it is the failure to discuss legacy planning that actually produces the most conflict. Difficult conversations cannot be avoided if our final wishes and those of our loved ones are to be fulfilled. We've all heard horror stories about how the mismanagement of estates has caused long-term rifts and fractures in family relationships. Much of this is caused by lack of communication and planning before death on how the distribution of assets is to be carried out.

> **Planning your legacy today will prevent conflict down the road that would be even more difficult to resolve in the absence of a plan.**

Although planning your legacy in advance may involve dealing with intense emotions, these crucial discussions about legacy planning can result in stronger relationships among your family members. Planning your legacy today will prevent conflict down the road that would be even more difficult to resolve in the absence of a plan.

Procrastination is another common obstacle. People often procrastinate legacy planning by rationalizing that there will always be time to deal with it later. We know for a sad fact that sometimes "later" comes sooner than we expect.

Part of procrastination is a fear of dealing with complication. It's always easier to put off what we imagine will take a lot of time and mental energy. But it's important to remember that any complicated task can be broken into manageable parts. As you begin sorting out and documenting the details of your life, you gain confidence knowing you are making it easier for your loved ones when your time does come. And you come to know the truth: Avoiding difficult decisions only postpones them — it doesn't eliminate them.

Death is one of life's most significant events and should be an integral part of everybody's financial plan. By documenting your final wishes and sharing what matters most to you, you'll be confident that your final wishes will be carried out as you desire and that your survivors won't have to deal with any unnecessary or unexpected details.

Creating Your Legacy Plan

Creating a legacy plan is a new endeavor for most people. For this reason it is ideal to work with a financial advisor who specializes in legacy planning. With their guidance and tools it is likely that you will create a superior plan. However, because legacy planning has not yet become a prominent expertise in the financial services industry, it may be very difficult to locate a good legacy advisor. So let me share some tips that will help you get started on your own.

1. Search the phrase "Plan Your Legacy" on the Internet to familiarize yourself with the concept and tools available.
2. Define what legacy planning means to you.
3. Brainstorm and begin with the end in mind — think big.
4. Identify any issues, concerns or questions.
5. Set a deadline for completion.
6. Put your legacy plan in writing — either on paper or stored electronically.
7. Notify the appropriate people that the plan exists.
8. Make sure to formalize the plan's delivery method. Much like assigning an executor to carry out a will, you need to come up with a solution that will ensure it gets into the right hands at the right time — otherwise it will just sit in the bottom of the drawer.
9. Keep your plan up to date.
10. Host an annual review with family members — the Friday after
11. Thanksgiving is always a good idea.
12. Review your legacy plan once a year.

The True Meaning of Life

What personal legacy will you leave behind? Will it be money — or something far more valuable? In the words of the legacy pioneer Scott Fithian, "Who will you be to the great-great-grandkids: the relative with all the money, or the soul who embraced charity even when his own luck was down?" In a world that is take, take, take, we need to stop and think about how much we can give and how our life will impact others. If you can truly make a difference to those you love and, ultimately, the world at large, then you can proudly say that your life has had meaning.

Mark Colgan
Plan Your Legacy, LLC
179 Sully's Trail, Suite 301
Pittsford, NY 14534
585.419.2270 (tel)
mcolgan@colgancapital.com
www.planyourlegacy.com

Mark Colgan is founder and president of Plan Your Legacy, LLC, a consulting firm specializing in legacy planning. His ultimate mission is to empower individuals to articulate and create a legacy plan that ultimately preserve their life values and final wishes.

Colgan is the creator of www.planyourlegacy.com, an easy-to-use, comprehensive Web site that expertly guides individuals through the legacy planning process. It gives individuals a place, structure and process for communicating their values, memories and final wishes, ultimately preserving their legacy and helping to ease the burden on survivors after death — giving them room to grieve, heal and celebrate their life. He is also the author of *The Survivors Assistance Handbook: A Guide for Financial Transition* and *The Personal Legacy Journal*, a workbook that allows individuals to pro-actively plan and document their legacy.

Colgan is also a frequent national speaker and an often-cited expert on legacy planning. His articles have been published in such national publications as *The Journal of Financial Planning, American Association of Individual Investors, The Director, ABA Journal*, and *Money Advisor*, a *Consumer Report's* publication.

9. Wealth Management and the Private Business Owner

Josh Patrick, CFP®, CLU, ChFC
Stage 2 Planning Partners

Many owners of private businesses go through their business lives working on projects as they occur. They don't make time to first understand what is important in their lives and then to develop action plans that deal with those things.

This is true for two reasons. First, many private business owners never take the time to gain clarity about what is important in their business and their personal life. Next, these individuals and others, perhaps like you, are so consumed with dealing with urgent matters that they — and maybe you — never get around to working on projects that are truly *important*, but not necessarily *urgent*.

We believe the projects that are important, but not urgent, are often where real value can be gained for you, your business and your family. We hope to give you some ideas about what we consider a good model for wealth management for the private business owner.

Wealth management is categorized into 11 areas. They are:

   1. Financial planning

2. Value creation in the business

3. Financing and capital structure

4. Risk management

5. Tax planning

6. Asset protection

7. Harvesting value from the business

8. Exit planning

9. Investment management

10. Wealth transfer planning

11. Legacy planning

We will consider each of these areas as we take our trip through wealth management for you, the private business owner.

I. The Financial Planning Process

Financial planning should be the starting place in a wealth management process for any private business owner. In this important preparatory stage, owners determine how much they need to live their daily life, plan for life stage expenses, such as educating children, and explore what they will need when it comes time to leave the business.

We use a tool with our private business owners called the Four Boxes of Financial Independence. This tool helps you, the private business owner, understand where your income will come from when you stop working.

The four boxes are:

1. Your business

2. Investment real estate from which you operate your business

3. Your 401(k) plan

4. Your other investments

When we start a conversation with many business owners, we ask the following question: When would you like to stop working? If the owner is more than 50 years old, we often hear five years as the ideal time frame for leaving the business. Usually owners don't know if they can afford to leave by then but have a sense that things will be different five years into the future, and figure that they will have accomplished whatever it takes to leave the business, even if they don't know what it will take.

We often work with business owners to help them understand that to leave the business when they want, they need a plan. And that plan will require diversification in investments outside of the core business. It is frequently the case that the core business won't provide enough income after sale or liquidation of the business. For example, a business that provides $200,000 per year for the owner while it's operating will usually provide only 20% of that income after it's sold.

A buyer will often pay between three and six times the annual earnings for your business. In the case above, this would provide the owner with $600,000 to $1,200,000 in capital before taxes. If we deduct 20% for taxes, the owner would be left with $480,000 to $960,000. Many financial planners think that a safe withdrawal rate from an investment for retirement is about 4% of the capital. Under the described scenario, the owner would be able to spend between $19,000 and $38,000 per year — far less than the $200,000 per year they were spending when they ran the business.

This means that our owner needs some other strategies to help him or her reach retirement income goals. Combining a regular savings plan with real estate ownership is usually enough to help the owner reach financial independence. It is not critical that the business owner fills every box, but diversification into three of the four enhances the likelihood of reaching financial independence in retirement.

Having a *personal* business plan — a plan that starts with the four boxes — is just as important as having a plan for your business. Many businesses and their owners do a good job planning for their business. They understand where the sales will come from and what expenses they will accrue during the year. They know how much capital they will need and where that capital will come from. But those same owners often don't do any personal planning.

Using the four boxes helps the owner provide a business plan for themselves as individuals. Having this personal plan in place will help you as a business owner understand whether your business can help you reach outcomes that are important for you.

Our four boxes tool is part of our Objective Review discovery process. We believe that if you don't do anything else, starting with a personal wealth plan lets you know whether the other things you are doing in your business and wealth accumulation activities make sense.

STOP & THINK

II. Value Creation in the Business

The first step in business owner wealth management is to create a financial plan that provides a blueprint for what you need for financial independence. The next step is to drive value creation in your business. For most owners of private businesses, this is either the first or second most important thing you can do to ensure that you will be able to leave your business in the manner you want, when you want.

Creating value in a business requires not only tactical excellence, but strategic excellence as well. When you have a business that is tactically excellent, it provides a nice job and pays a very nice salary. If you were to step away from the business for an extended period of time, it probably wouldn't work as well and may even go out of business.

This brings us to the first thing you need to do to create value in your business. You must make yourself operationally irrelevant in your business. By doing this, you now have gone past creating a job for yourself to having a business that can run whether you are there or not. Once you have done this, you now have a business that others would want to own.

> Creating value in a business requires not only tactical excellence, but strategic excellence as well.

Making yourself operationally irrelevant in your business also allows you to start moving toward a Stage 2 business. This is where the business goes past operational excellence and achieves strategic excellence as well. For a business to make this transition, the owner of the business must learn not only to think strategically, but also to act strategically. We find that most business owners are good at thinking strategically but never have the time to put those thoughts into actions.

When business owners make themselves operationally irrelevant, they create a personal capacity for changing what they do at work. The owner can now spend time on strategic activities which can increase the value of the business in two ways. First, the profits and cash flow from the business should improve, and second, a potential buyer will not only pay for the cash flow the business creates, but also the technology for creating the additional cash flow.

For example, if the owner of the business learns not only what the intellectual capital of the business is, but also how to charge for that intellectual capital, they can sometimes double or triple the value of the business. If the owner learns how to segment the businesses customer base and only allow its sales department to sell to the most profitable customers, the business value will increase. If the owner of the business learns to segment the business into profitable niches and then finds ways of finding new niches, they will increase the value of the business, often by a factor of two or three times.

Increasing the value of your business requires tactical excellence first — that is the price to play in the world of business value creation. Once you do this, then strategic excellence compounds the possibilities for value creation. With strategic excellence you will develop the personal capacity to spend time on things that are important, but not urgent. This is the green zone of time management, where you are controlling your business and your business is not controlling you.

III. Financing and Capital Structure

Many private business owners are intimidated — sometimes to the point of immobility — by their banks. When I look at their balance sheets, I scratch my head in wonder. Usually further conversation with the business owner uncovers the reason for their fear: at some point in their past, their business didn't perform well and the bank came down on them. Often the owner thought the bank was about to put them out of business. Even though the company financials have recovered, the owner has not.

Your bank is a supplier — I have to remind these business owners that the bank is just a supplier to their company. The relationship is important, sure, but you should work for the best deal that is in your best interest. You can be certain that your bank will work to make a deal that is in their best interest, just like every other supplier you deal with.

Just as you manage your other supplier relationships, you should manage your bank relationships. It's important to understand how the bank thinks and to understand the need for capital within your company. If your company is strong, you are in a good position to set the terms of engagement with your bank. When this happens, you often have too much cash in your company or aren't using debt in an effective manner. If your company is not as profitable as you like or your company is expanding very rapidly, your bank may be less cooperative. In this case, you must understand how your bankers think and learn how to communicate with them in a manner that they understand.

STOP & THINK

Step One: Understand your balance sheet — Most of the companies we work with either have too much or too little debt in their company. Business owners often don't understand what the proper use of debt is. Those with too little debt will keep large amounts of cash in the company and pay for everything with cash. Emotionally this is a great way to live. However, when it comes to getting an adequate return on your business, it often leads to not having money in the right place when it's time to leave your business.

There are several formulas that are crucial for understanding the capitalization of your business. The two formulas that deal with effective use of capital are return on assets and return on equity. Your bank will be very interested in knowing your debt-to-equity ratio as well as your cash flow coverage for your loans.

Step Two: Understand the cost of capital — Leaving money in your business is very expensive. If you use an appropriate amount of debt, you will be able to remove money from your business and use this capital in other ways. If your business is well run, your bank will be more than happy to loan you the money that you took out of your business.

Capital invested in your company is very expensive. Capital that you can borrow from your bank is relatively inexpensive. The challenge is that many successful private business owners are debt-averse. These owners could dramatically increase their business returns if they learned how to use debt appropriately in their business. For example, it is easy and inexpensive to borrow money for equipment, since equipment loans are secured by the equipment. So it is better to borrow for this purpose and keep your cash for another day.

Step Three: Become financially literate — More often than not, the business owners we work with don't understand the financial ratios that drive their business. Because of this, they don't know if they are using their business cash in a manner that helps them reach their goals. Banks have guidelines for each business they deal with. Talk to your bankers and find out what they are expecting from you.

Understanding how banks think about your business and knowing the range of your business financial ratios can have a large effect on your business and on the independence you might want in the future. We recommend you have a conversation with your financial advisor or wealth manager about your particular situation and not only learn what your banker is looking for, but also find the sweet spot for your own business.

Step Four: Review your banking relationships — Finally, remember that a bank is a supplier, nothing more and nothing less. At least every few years, you should have a conversation with other banks that serve your industry and your community to find out what they have to offer. You may be surprised to learn that different banks have different priorities, and that their goals change over time, sometimes to your benefit.

Still, it is true that a good bank is as beneficial as any other good supplier. A strong relationship is worth a lot. Just don't let false claims of relationship keep you from knowing when it is time to make a change.

IV. Risk Management

Most of the world has a relatively easy time managing the risks in life. Most people have a job, a home and a family, all of which bring risks to manage. Risk management for the private business owner is much more difficult. Not only do you have to manage the insurance coverage for your personal and business risk, you also need to have plans in place in case the worst should happen.

> Many risks can be insured. ... However, just having insurance coverage may not be enough.

Plan for the worst — As the business owner, you need to work with your key employees to develop a list of the five to ten worst things that could happen to your business. Once this list is assembled, call a meeting with your key managers, your liability insurance agent, your health insurance agent, your life and disability insurance agent, your attorney and your CPA.

First, review the list to determine which things would have the potential to put you out of business. These are the risks you and the assembled team should concentrate on.

Many risks can be insured. For example, you can purchase insurance for personal injury in case the products you make injure someone. However, just having insurance coverage may not be enough. You will also want to have plans in place to protect the reputation of your company.

We've all heard about companies where someone is badly injured by a product or service the company provides. Often with smaller businesses, this can mean the end of the business. The business may have had adequate insurance, but the owner didn't have a plan to make sure the public knows the problem has been fixed. It's having this plan in place that can mean the difference between success and failure in a risk management plan.

Coordinate your personal and business risk — We often see that business owners have one agent for business insurance and another agent for personal insurance. There is nothing wrong with this as long as the coverage is coordinated between the two. Most business owners we know don't bother with this coordination if they use two agents.

One of the most important types of coverage you can purchase is an umbrella policy, which typically has a limit of $2 million or more over your basic policy coverage. Umbrella policies all have requirements of underlying coverage before they will kick in. You need to make sure that your underlying coverage for your personal and business life is adequate. The only way to do this is to coordinate coverage between the companies you use.

If you don't have one agency covering both your business and personal life, you will need to get in writing from both agents that they have reviewed your policies and believe that your coverage is adequate and complete.

Have ownership for the right policy in the right place — We often see life insurance inside the business that has been purchased to protect the owner's family should the owner die. In our view, this is a mistake. If the owner dies, the bank will have first claim on the insurance proceeds, not the owner's family, as they intended. Insurance purchased for family protection needs proper ownership. Proper ownership is by your spouse, who will need the cash if you're not around.

A sad fact about private business is that most businesses will not exist if the owner is not available for coordinating day-to-day operations of that business. A way to protect your personal risk is to make sure that insurance is owned and placed correctly to have the effect your business requires.

V. Tax Planning

One of the largest costs you face as a private business owner is the cost of taxes. You have taxes coming from all directions. Sometimes it even feels that all you do is run your business for the benefit of various taxing authorities.

Chapter 9. The Private Business Owner

One of the advantages of running a private business is that you have the opportunity to use legitimate tax deductions that favor you as well as your business.

Understand where you are taxed — You need to know where you are paying taxes. For example, you might be organized as an LLC and choose to be taxed as a partnership. In this situation, you will pay Social Security and Medicare taxes on 100% of the income your share of the LLC produces. If instead you choose to be taxed as a Sub Chapter S Corporation, you would be taxed only on the portion of the income you take as W2 income. This can often save you thousands of dollars on an annual basis.

Use multiple entities when appropriate — Having your assets owned by appropriate legal entities is important not only for asset protection, but also for tax planning. If you own real estate, you don't want it inside either a Sub Chapter S Corporation or a C Corporation. You will want it inside a partnership or an LLC that is taxed as a partnership. This will allow you maximum flexibility when it comes time to sell or exchange that property in the future.

Often you will want to have a C Corporation and a Sub Chapter S Corporation for providing different services to your clients. We often see a C Corporation used as a general partner for real estate and the Sub Chapter S Corporation for assets within a corporation. This is an excellent asset protection strategy that doubles as a very good tax planning method.

C Corporations have items that can be deducted as normal business expenses that Sub Chapter S Corporations don't. Working with your tax professionals to understand the difference between the two is important.

Take all legal deductions — Every December we receive calls asking about deductions our clients can take to help limit their taxes. First, make this call to your advisors in June and you have a chance of making the deductions legal. Second, make sure you ask your tax professionals about anything that might be construed as a deduction.

One of the benefits of owning and operating your own company is that some of your annual expenses can be run as legitimate business expenses. This can save you as much as $80 per $100 that you spend on any item. If you spend $100 on an item and you can use it as a legitimate business expense, you spend $100 for that item only. If instead you purchase the same item from personal funds, you will first have to earn enough money to pay the taxes and then use what you have leftover to purchase the item. If you are in a 30%

tax bracket, this means that you will need to earn $143 to pay for that $100 item.

Tax planning must make sense — The goal is not just to pay fewer taxes. The goal is to use your money in an appropriate and smart manner. If you need an item for your business, then you should plan how to purchase that item at the lowest possible tax cost. If the business does not need that item, then just purchasing it to save taxes will cost you money.

Some owners attempt to save taxes by not reporting all their sales. The IRS is on to this and has the right to put people in jail. Tax management is not about cheating on taxes — it's about minimizing your tax bite in all legal and rational ways.

VI. Asset Protection

We live in a litigious society. If we haven't been sued, we certainly know someone in our business community who has been sued, often with disastrous results. This section deals with the basics of asset protection. It will cover the easy things to do that might help protect you if the worst happens.

Have a plan — The first step we always suggest to our business owners is that they first determine what are the largest risks facing their business. We then suggest that they craft a disaster plan for what they would do if any of these events happens.

We often talk about being proactive versus reactive in running a business. If you are being proactive, your plan is ready before the event happens. If you do this, there is a better than even chance that you will come out of the event whole. If you don't have a plan, then you are not only dealing with the problem, but you are also trying to figure out what to do on the fly. This is where mistakes happen.

We suggest that as you assemble this plan you include your accountant, your lawyer, your insurance agents and key managers of your company. All have different viewpoints and information you will need in assembling your plan.

Use corporate and asset protection structures — Over and over again, I'm amazed by how many owners of private businesses don't have at least one corporation for their business. In high-risk businesses or high-risk parts of the country, you will want to have several corporations that protect various parts of your business. If you are in a business where professional liability is not protected by a corporation, you should work with an asset protection specialist who will help you struture the ownership of your assets in such a manner that it will be tougher for creditors to get you and your assets if the worst should happen.

We often suggest that contracts should be owned by one corporation and hard assets should be owned by another corporation. For example, if you are a construction company, the equipment you use is owned by one company. This company would lease the use of those assets to your operating company. This would protect the hard assets, or at least make it more difficult for creditors to attach those assets.

You must plan early — There is a term in the asset protection world: fraudulent conveyance. You don't want to be caught by this concept. Simply stated, it means that if you transfer assets knowing that a lawsuit is going to happen, you will have those assets drawn back into any settlement.

For this reason, you must plan early if you expect to protect your assets from creditors. The name of the game in asset protection is often making it difficult and expensive for your creditors to prevail. You might end up paying some money, but that money will likely be less than if you had done no planning.

> You must plan early if you expect to protect your assets from creditors.

VII. Harvesting Value from Your Business

You've started a business and have made it through the very tough start-up phase. You've created some predictability in your business. Now it's time to start getting some of that value out of the business. This is where you start thinking about diversification, not for safety, but to expand the possibilities of what you can do later in life.

In our section on financial planning we talked about the kind of diversification that allows you to leave your business. Now let's discuss a few strategies that you can use to extract cash from your business now, while you are still actively engaged in it.

Buy some real estate — The first step in harvesting value is to own the real estate your business occupies. You are paying rent, and if possible, you should pay that rent to yourself. We often see that when the owner of the business leaves their business, the rental income their building produces is worth more than the business itself.

STOP & THINK

You will need to take some money out of your business for your down payment. You will also want to have the building amortized for no more than 15 years. This will allow you to have a building with no mortgage and plenty of cash when it comes time to leave your business.

Look at your 401(k) plan — For many business owners, the next logical step is to look at their 401(k) plans to make sure they are putting the maximum away for themselves. If you are already putting 3% into your plan for your employees; you can often increase the amount you are putting away for yourself. If you can add another 2% for your employees, you can often save as much as $50,000 for you and your spouse on an annual basis.

Strong savings in your 401(k) plan can often make the difference between leaving your business on your terms or having to go to work for somebody else after you sell or close your business. We call this strategy pre-funding your buyout. Many businesses have little or no market value when it comes time to sell. But if the owners pre-fund their buyout with present cash, they are able to set their own terms when it's time to leave the business.

Managing debt for other investments — We have already covered managing the amount of cash and debt you have in your business. Understanding how debt works and why it is important to have enough — but not too much — cash in your business helps you find the cash for diversification into other investments.

Those other investments could be a Roth IRA, stocks, bonds, real estate or even passive interests in other businesses. Money that you are leaving in your company could keep you from profiting from other opportunities. Your business is a great value generator, yes, but what other opportunities are you passing up?

You need to do an opportunity cost analysis of leaving cash in the business versus using that cash for other investment opportunities. First, you must make sure your company balance sheet is solid. Most business owners have this instinct. But once that is accomplished, leaving more cash in the business can be damaging.

The purpose of harvesting value is to provide options for the future. You have a nice lifestyle that allows you a good standard of living. You want to protect that lifestyle in the future. Diversification can add options, and that is what harvesting value is all about.

VIII. Exit Planning

In his book *How to Run Your Business So You Can Leave It In Style*, attorney John Brown discusses exit planning and uses a seven-step process for planning your eventual exit from your business. His process includes:

- Establishing Owners Objectives — Financial Planning
- Establishing Business Value — Value World Analysis
- Building Business Value — Value Creation
- Selling to a Third Party — Value Harvesting
- Transferring to Management or Family — Value Harvesting
- Developing a Contingency Plan for the Business — Risk Management
- Family Wealth Preservation Planning — Wealth Transfer

From the list above you see that the exit planning process according to John Brown involves five of the 11 areas of wealth management for the private business owner. Planning for a successful exit involves working with an advisor or advisors who have an interdisciplinary understanding of what needs to be done for that successful exit to happen.

But first, the main question — I find that when working with a private business owner on the exit planning process, one question must be answered before any other. That question is, "Should I keep the business and operate it as a cash-generating machine or should I sell the business, change my day-to-day activities and live on passive income from the capital value I realize from my business?" Or, to put it simply, "Should I keep or sell the business? And if I sell, to whom should I sell it and by what means?"

The keep-or-sell question will help you concentrate on the appropriate sections of a wealth management process that helps you achieve your goals. Remember, all the advisors you work with during this process will have an agenda, and you will need to drive your agenda and make sure you are working toward the outcomes that are important for you.

The sales process — Suppose you, as a business owner, have decided that you want to transition out of your business. If you have created a business with enterprise value (a business that someone else wants to own) you have several options as to who will be the next owner.

STOP & THINK

The three main options are selling to an outsider, selling to your managers or passing the business to family members. In many cases you will want to examine all three at the same time before making a decision about the option you ultimately want to pursue.

Understanding value worlds — Private businesses have several market values at the same time. The difference in those values can be huge. For example, the liquidation value of a business might be $500,000 while the strategic value of the business might be $5 million. It is a critical part of the exit planning process to understand the different value worlds and how they fit in with your long-term personal economic plans.

We suggest that you value your business based on three or four different value worlds. This will help you make a more intelligent decision about which channel you will ultimately pursue when it comes time to transition out of your business.

The advisory world — When selling your business we believe it's crucial that you use outside advisors who understand the process. These advisors should have the ability to help you through the process, and they should also have a clear understanding of the different sales opportunities you have.

It is rare to find an advisor who understands and is conversant in all the transfer methods, so it is that much more important that you, as the private business owner, stay in control of your goals. This means you first need to be clear about what you want out of the transfer and then stay true to that as you go through the process.

IX. Investment Management

Investment management is the traditional core of wealth management or financial planning as practiced today. Most financial planners concentrate more on investment management than on any other portion of the wealth management or financial planning process. They also earn most of their money from investment management.

Asset allocation should lead the conversation — We believe that investment management conversations should always start with a conversation about asset allocation. Research has shown that slightly more than 90% of your investment return will be determined by the allocation you choose for your investments. Approximately 4% of your return is achieved by the actual selection of stocks and bonds.[1]

Concentrate on volatility — The next portion of your investment strategy should concentrate on the projected volatility of your portfolio. We believe that managing downside risk is much more important than concentrating on upside potential.

If you have $1,000 and have a 100% gain in your investment, you will now have $2,000. If you take $2,000 and have a 50% reduction in value, you will once again have $1,000. For this reason we believe that concentrating on a strategy that helps minimize downside risk is important for the long-term health of your portfolio.

Core and Satellite Investing — The third area of concentration for investment management should be on developing a core and satellite strategy. Typically, the core investments you have are stocks and bonds. Here you will concentrate on using cost-effective investment vehicles such as index funds or exchange-traded funds (ETFs). We believe that in the core section of managing your investments, passive strategies provide more long-term value than active investment management.

Satellite investment strategies will include those stock sectors where active management can add value. We believe the satellite sector of your investments should include alternative investments that are designed to provide regular returns no matter what happens in the broad market.

The goal of a core-satellite investment strategy is to provide you with positive inflation-adjusted returns that have lower-than-average volatility.

Understand the movement to passive income — The fourth part of an investment strategy for owners of private business is to understand the impact of moving from an active income situation (you receive a paycheck from your business) to one where a major portion of your income will now come from the returns your investments provide. We often suggest that business owners have some active income in the portfolio, frequently from the investment real estate from which you run your business. You may decide to sell your business for many reasons. We regularly suggest that you keep ownership of the real estate you owned while running the business. The income from this real estate can become important in

---

[1] Gary P. Brinson, Brian D. Singer, and Gilbert L. Beebower, *"Determinants of Portfolio Performance II: An Update."* The predecessor study, *"Determinants of Portfolio Performance."* Brinson, Hood & Beebower, *Financial Analysts Journal*, 1986; Brinson, Singer & Beebower, *Financial Analysts Journal*, 1991

meeting cash flow needs after you sell your business.

Choosing an investment advisor also involves issues of trust. We suggest you ask yourself if the person you've chosen is someone you feel comfortable trusting with your financial future. Often the decisions you and your advisor make will have a meaningful impact — either positive or negative — on your financial future.

X. Wealth Transfer Process/Legacy Planning

Most private business owners stay away from wealth transfer or estate planning issues until they sell or have a liquidity event with their business. The reason for this is that wealth transfer planning often has irrevocable transfers attached to the process. Until you, the owner of the private business, actually have the cash in your hands, you don't often believe your business value is real.

When you need to do estate planning — Most of the time estate or wealth transfer planning are not high-priority items, at least not beyond the basics. It is necessary to do basic estate planning as part of risk management and asset protection for your family. You will want to have your assets pass to your spouse or significant other and you will want to have an orderly transfer of your business if you are not around to run the business.

Estate planning is also crucial when you plan to transfer your business to your children or other family members. Not having done adequate wealth transfer planning can unravel the plans you have made with respect to who will run and control the company in the future.

Some estate planning basics — You will want to think about how much of your estate you want to go to your spouse or significant other and how much of your estate you want to go to your children or other heirs. You will also want to understand how to use the unified credit for each of you to take maximum advantage of the estate tax exclusion the government gives you.

Basic estate planning is about managing risk. You want to make sure your children will be educated and your spouse has a reasonable chance to live his or her life in an appropriate manner. You also want to make sure your children don't squabble about your estate after you pass on.

Working with a competent estate planning team will help you achieve basic risk management needs with ease. The core team we recommend should include an attorney who specializes in tax and estate law, an insurance agent who understands planning opportunities for the private business owner, and a CPA who understands the needs of the business after you're gone.

Advanced planning opportunities — If the business is a large one and you want to pass it to the next generation of managers, or if you've sold your business and your estate value is more than $7 million, you will probably want to engage in more advanced planning to limit the estate taxes your family pays. You also will want to control who has influence in the business and make sure your children are treated fairly for estate distribution issues.

You often will run into the alphabet soup of estate planning at this point in your life. Estate planning professionals throw around terms such as GRAT (Grantor Retained Annuity Trust), NIMCRUT (Net-Income with Make-Up charitable Remainder Trust), CRUT (Charitable Remainder Unitrust) or Defective Trusts. You may even decide to use some of these techniques to help you achieve your goals.

The key to advanced estate planning is to have clearly delineated goals for what you are trying to accomplish. After your goals are established, you should use a seasoned team of professionals to put your plans in place. Your wealth manager will play a crucial role in assembling and coordinating the work of the team.

Conclusion

The wealth management process is an interdisciplinary one. Successful management comes from working with your entire advisory team. Typically, you will choose one of your team members to be your wealth manager. This person will be responsible for coordinating the management of your wealth with great input and direction from you.

Not only does your wealth manager need to have general knowledge and an excellent rolodex for all the areas listed above, but they also must be able to help you develop your mission, vision, values and goals. This person is the one who will be responsible for helping you design and leave a legacy that lives long after you do.

You not only want to preserve, protect and enhance your assets, but you also want to preserve and pass on the wisdom you've developed over the years. An effective wealth manager will help you achieve your goals and help you pass on the legacy you desire to those who are important in your life.

Josh Patrick, CFP®, CLU, ChFC
Stage 2 Planning Partners
20 Kimball Ave., Suite 201
South Burlington, VT 05403
802.846.1264 or 877.880.5112 (tel)
www.stage2planning.com

Josh Patrick, CFP®, CLU, ChFC, has spent his adult life running and building businesses. For the first 20 years of his business career, he was President and operated Patrick's Food Service. From a company with one employee Josh built the company to four branch operations with 90 employees.

During Josh's tenure in the food service business he served as President of the New York State Vending Association, was Education Director for the National Vending Association and, in that capacity, developed several courses on financial and people management skills. He currently writes a bi-monthly column on maintaining financial wealth for an industry magazine. In 1995 he sold his vending operation and started working in the financial services industry, first, for a large mutual insurance company, and since 1997 as President of his own firm, The Patrick Group, Inc.

Josh specializes in working with closely held business owners on a variety of concentrated issues that are unique to owners of private firms. Among these are risk assessment, cash flow planning, investment planning, retirement plan design, estate planning, succession planning and family business strategies.

Josh has spoken for many national trade associations and specializes in helping owners of closely held businesses develop plans that improve their personal satisfaction and bottom line in their business. Josh presently is a member of Partners Financial, an insurance producer group. He also is a member of the National Association of Life Underwriters, the Financial Planning Association, the Million Dollar Roundtable and the Advanced Association of Life Underwriters. He holds a B.A. from Boston University and has the Chartered Financial Consultant and Chartered Life Underwriter designations from the American College. He is a licensee and holder of the Certified Financial Planner™ designation and a Registered Representative and Investment Advisor Representative with NFP Securities, Inc.

10. The Definition of a Trusted Advisory Firm

Stephanie Enright, MS, CFP®
Enright Premier Wealth Advisors

A trusted advisory firm should be composed of well-qualified, experienced members. They can, at different times, be for clients a sounding board, reflector of concerns, satisfier of needs, confessor, mentor and, occasionally, even a virtual punching bag to receive good, bad and, sometimes, impractical concepts.

An excerpt from a long-ago conversation between Bill Gates and Warren Buffett gives a view of this:

Gates: *It's important to have someone who you totally trust, who is totally committed, who shares your vision, and yet who has a little bit different set of skills and who also acts as something of a check on you. Some of the ideas you run by him, you know he's going to say, "Hey wait a minute, have you thought about this and that?" The benefit of sparking off somebody who's got that kind of brilliance is that it not only makes business more fun, but it really leads to a lot of success."*

Buffett: *"I've had a partner like that, Charlie Munger, for a lot of years, and it does for me exactly what Bill is talking about. You have to calibrate with Charlie, though, because Charlie says everything I do is dumb, I take that as an affirmative vote."*

1 The Trusted Advisor, by David H. Maister, Charles H. Green & Robert M. Galford, copyright 2000

Thus, the chosen firm must provide exceptional ongoing value to clients. This requires in-house professional knowledge and services in business, technical, financial and investment arenas while considering their more subjective and personal issues. Even more important are each member's abilities to understand and be responsive and communicative while acting ethically and being truly involved with clients' varied beliefs, concerns and needs.

All advisors and clients will have some flaws, but it is the advisors' ability to support the clients' strengths and assist in overriding their weaknesses combined with confidentiality that is critical.

To summarize the clients' viewpoint about a trusted advisor:

- Likes to understand us
- Helps us reach clear, viable decisions
- Has enough firm depth to be there for the long haul
- Can relate to others who are of importance to us, whether in business or personally
- Helps translate complex issues
- Has the intelligence and aptitude to assist in making smart team decisions with us

Trusted Advisors Provide Varied Services

All affluent individuals and families have three aspects to their assets: financial, social and emotional. The financial aspect is the most commonly understood and addressed of the three. This is what has been accumulated in the past and continues to accumulate in the present and future. Major blocks of time and energy are/have been devoted to the "wealth objective." It is the most impersonal of the three aspects. Assets and liabilities are not about people. They are about things owned by people. This financial aspect is very well defined. Most affluent people have an accurate idea of net worth. Many traditional advisors are interested in, and are experts in, "just the economic facts," which doesn't make them uncaring or incompetent. They are doing the job they were trained to do and feel comfortable in performing. A true wealth advisor must offer excellent investment advice and portfolio management as an essential part of their services. They are, however, limiting themselves.

There are two other vital aspects to a family's wealth. First is the social aspect, which entails how their wealth is used and directed for the good of themselves, those they love, friends, institutions and causes they care about. A truly rich life comes from incorporating caring and implementation with an ongoing plan and direction. This can best be understood if the advisor conducts an initial in-depth exploratory meeting with clients and, later, includes family and business associates who are vital to their lives.

The other aspect is the emotional/ spiritual, which is the most intimate. Here is where questions are explored that cannot be answered by looking at a financial statement, balance sheet or legal documents. Life is more than the accumulation of money or the avoidance of taxes. Life is about having an influence, building relationships and making a difference. To counsel clients in accomplishing this takes most advisors out of their comfort zones. But an advisor who can help facilitate what the clients truly need and want can join with them as a long-term trusted advisor.

On a less subjective level, services that can be provided or coordinated could be:

I. For the Closely Held Business Owners

1. Reviews of their business entity choices for possible change:

- Sole proprietorship
- Partnership
- Corporation
- Limited liability company

2. Consideration of employee benefits offered:

- Fringe benefits
- Qualified retirement plans
- Defined benefit plans
- Defined contribution plans
- Simplified retirement plans
- Evaluating retirement choices

3. Key Employee Perks:

- Deferred compensation plans

- Stock bonus and stock option plans
- Life insurance (as a benefit)

4. Details of Exit Strategies and Succession Planning

- Succession planning
- Business valuation
- Selling to co-owners
- Selling to employees
- Giving to family members
- Selling to outsiders

II. For Business Executives

- Compensation packages now and future
- Executive perks
- Stock option plans
- Career path choices
- Tax analysis
- Investment management choices within retirement and other benefit plans
  - » Are plans well structured?
  - » Can outside advisors be used?
  - » Retirement Choices:
  - » Age, part-time employment possibilities
  - » Amortization vs. lump sum
  - » Insurance benefits: life, medical for family as well as individual
  - » Other post-retirement benefits: social, financial, and personal

III. For the Already-Retired Individuals and Widows/Widowers

- Risk-adjusted investment management
- Timing and choice of income withdrawal
- Health, long-term care and life insurance
- Tax avoidance planning
- Benefiting children and grandchildren

- Estate planning
- Referrals to outside professionals for health, social and psychological requirements, to a real estate professional for home changes, to schools for continuing education, and as needed to a well-screened, ethical community of outside resources for personal, family and other interests and needs.

Objective and Subjective Qualifications that Should be Provided to Prospective Clients

First, the professional planners' and advisors' credentials/ affiliations and designations held by firm members should be reviewed. There is a multitude of varied designations, so it is critical to distinguish among those that are professionally recognized versus others that do not require the same depth of study, experience and continuing education. Unfortunately, there is an alphabet soup of these.

The most well-known and legitimate credentials are Doctors of Law (LLD), Certified Public Accountants (CPA), Master's in Business Administration (MBA) from a known university, Certified Financial Planner™ (CFP®), Chartered Financial Analyst (CFA), Certified Investment

> Have the advisors clarify how their training and designations will serve your particular situation.

Management Consultant (CIMA), Chartered Financial Consultant (ChFC) and Registered Investment Advisor (RIA). CFPs have the important subsets of financial planning and wealth advisory; with additional study including investment planning, insurance, income taxation, retirement benefits and estate planning. They must have 30-plus hours of continuing education and testing every two years. CFAs are specialists in investment management. Their credential demands professional employment in the field and a three-year course with an extensive exam at the end of each year. ChFC is a credential given by the American College. Its strongest focus is on the field of insurance. RIA is a designation for investment advisory and fiduciaries. There certainly are other designations. Be sure to check what is required in time, depth of knowledge and continuing education to receive and maintain any specific credential.

In addition, have the advisors clarify how their training and designations will serve your particular situation. Have them give precise descriptions of past and existing client situations in which they were able to utilize the ongoing knowledge their qualifications gave them. (Details on contacting each organization that issues and maintains designations are at the end of this chapter.)

In-depth, sophisticated experience is a requirement for top-level client input. It is imperative to explore what actual hands-on experience the advisors have with certain types of clients and their issues. For example, a business executive with a firm who has an Employee Stock Ownership Plan (ESOP) is contemplating retirement. He or she will need expertise in the various ways of handling an ESOP rollover to avoid immediate taxation and loss of principal. For a real estate investor who is considering a sale or exchange of real estate, expertise in the field plus relationships with 1031 Exchange facilitators is imperative. A tax analysis of depreciation and possible sale will be required as well.

If you are working with a wealth management team, investigate the length and depth of time and varied experiences each member can demonstrate and verify.

Wealth advisory can be very involved, so request references from both existing clients and from other professionals. Check references and delve deep in conversations with those given as referrals. Experienced, competent advisors will provide a comprehensive list of names for clients. Probe into what type of services they have received from the firm. Are their needs being met? Disclose to client referrals what, in general, your situation is. Find out how you can realize beneficial results from the experiences of other clients who may have similar circumstances. You can also ask about the services they are receiving via mail, the Internet, by phone, and in one-on-one or group meetings. Is this the type of communication they had hoped for? If so, ask for a few specific examples.

Your issues may not be exactly like another client's, but there should be enough similarities to see if this is the team for your situation. To use a social analogy, if you need a highly precise, detailed review of numerous complicated, closely held business issues, a good advisor with an excellent personality may not be sufficient to handle your needs, even though he or she may be extremely charming.

It is imperative that financial advisors state in writing that they act as fiduciaries. A fiduciary is both ethically and legally obligated to always put the clients' best interests ahead of their own. The importance of this cannot be over-emphasized. There are many good people working for firms who are obligated to offer their firm's product to clients whether or not they are good when compared with similar available offerings.

To summarize and simplify, here are the direct questions you should ask a prospective advisor:

1. Who are you?
2. What do you do?
3. Why do you do what you do?
4. How do you do what you do?
5. Who have you done it for?
6. What makes you different?
7. Why should I do business with you?
8. How are you compensated?
9. Who will my contacts be?

Professional Collaboration

Professional team development and collaboration is essential for wealth advisors. No firm or team can have a high level of internal expertise in all the analysis and solutions required for high performance. As an example, if our firm was a travel advisor and our clients wanted an effortless flight to New York plus a lavish reception for their daughter's engagement there, this would require specialized knowledge of travel and all the details. Obviously, this would require very different expertise and contacts than if the request from the client was to research and identify the best medical facility and physician for an in-depth examination, treatment and follow-up care for the wife of an executive client. She has been diagnosed with a rare gastrointestinal blockage. The local hospital staff has neither a properly qualified physician nor the resources to recommend the proper treatment leading to a cure for this rare illness. Diverse past experiences, different critical contacts and implementation skills are required when an advisor teams with other experts. There will be variances in areas of expertise, costs and time frames needed for top results to be produced. The trusted advisor is responsible for coordination of the team plus interpretation of recom-

Partial Sale of Business

A business owner was contemplating a sale of the tool and dye assembly part of his manufacturing firm. He had family members as employees and was concerned about their future careers. He also needed to decide if he should also sell the firm-owned building in which the assembly function was housed. Perhaps he should retain it, lease it back to the new buyers and have ongoing income. There was a need for expert consultation on valuations, taxation, real estate management, best legal and business sale format, cash management, estate changes and employment considerations. This required a coordinated team of attorneys, a CPA, a real estate brokerage, an employment consultant and personal advisor to the family. After completion of the initial transaction, further planning sessions for the client and spouse were required to explore estate taxation, insurance, family charitable intents and future retirement plans.

Clients need someone to help them choose the right planning tools, techniques and teams to help them efficiently and economically achieve the optimum results in each varied situation. Also, the advisor must be adaptable to working cooperatively with clients and outside professionals.

mendations for the client.

Client Objectives

Financial Goals—Research has shown that the following are goals of more than 50% of affluent individuals throughout various stages of their lives:

- Ensure a comfortable standard of living during retirement
- Maintain current standard of living
- Build a sizeable investment portfolio
- Minimize tax burden
- Travel extensively
- Possibly buy a second home and vacation
- Protect estate against taxes
- Finance children's or grandchildren's college education
- Transfer wealth to family members
- Protect family against premature death or disability
- Make charitable contributions to chosen causes

Comfort with Non Traditional Investments — Many affluent clients do not have a high comfort level with investments such as:

- Hedge funds
- Private equity
- Venture capital

- Offshore holdings

Risk Attitudes — However, less than 40% of affluent investors prefer a guaranteed rate of return for most of their investments. Risk perception and management vary both with the personal and business background of clients. Business owners often have a predisposition to invest in their own business because it is a known quantity and, to some degree, manageable. They are not concerned with over-concentration in one asset area. Other investors prefer a concentration in real estate because of its appreciation potential and tax benefits. Some affluent clients like the barbell approach. On one end are risky holdings such as venture capital, private equity or second trust deeds, and on the other end they'll hold safer investments like CDs and cash, along with well-rated treasury, municipal or corporate bonds.

The Advisory Approach Exhibit #1

STOP & THINK

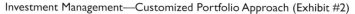

Investment Management—Customized Portfolio Approach (Exhibit #2)

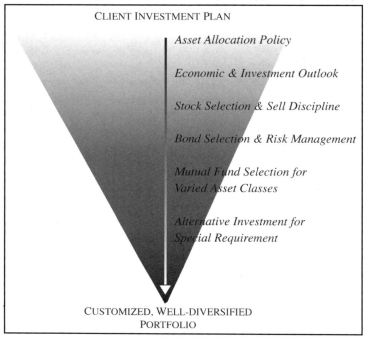

CLIENT INVESTMENT PLAN

Asset Allocation Policy

Economic & Investment Outlook

Stock Selection & Sell Discipline

Bond Selection & Risk Management

Mutual Fund Selection for Varied Asset Classes

Alternative Investment for Special Requirement

CUSTOMIZED, WELL-DIVERSIFIED
PORTFOLIO

It is important to check out any professional that you are contemplating working with, especially to investigate if they have any legal or ethical violations. Additionally, registered investment advisors have a fiduciary duty to work only in the best interest of their clients. They must disclose any conflicts of interest. Following is a list of sources through which to investigate.

1. Certified Financial Planner Board of Standards, Inc.
   Tel: (888) 237-6275
   Website: www.cfp.net

2. National Association of Securities Dealers
   Tel: (301) 590-6500   www.nasd.com
   Broker Check Hotline: (800) 289-9999

3. Municipal Securities Board
   Tel: (703) 797-6600
   Website: www.msrb.com

4. Chartered Financial Analyst Institute
   Tel: (800) 247-8132
   Website: www.cfainstitute.org

5. U.S. Securities and Exchange Commission
   Tel: (202)942-8088
   Website: www.sec.gov

Each registered investment advisory firm must provide their ADV form to clients. To view a firm's ADV form, visit www.adviserinfo.sec.gov.

Left: Derek H. Holman
Center: Stephanie V. Enright
Right: Brian E. Parker

Stephanie V. Enright
Enright Premier Wealth Advisors
21515 Hawthorne Blvd., Suite 1200
Torrance, CA 90503
800.272.2328 (tel)
senright@enrightpremier.com
www.enrightpremier.com

Stephanie V. Enright, MS, CFP®, is President of Enright Premier Wealth Advisors in Torrance, California. With more than 25 years of serving institutions, non-profit organizations, businesses, and affluent individuals, Stephanie and her co-directors, Derek Holman, CFP® and Brian Parker, CFP® specialize in financial planning, wealth advisory, and investment management. Their mission is to understand each client's unique situation. Stephanie's highly credentialed 18-member staff of CFPs and CFAs enables the firm to develop customized plans to achieve clients' specific goals and objectives.

The firm offers services on a fee basis; thus, providing true objectivity. They do not manufacture investment products, or offer internal investment banking. Eliminating conflicts of interest is an essential part of maintaining a client-first relationship. As fiduciaries, they believe it is their responsibility to understand what each client wants to accomplish, and to manage their investments to achieve the desired outcome.

A few of Enright's accolades include: Honored by Bloomberg's *Wealth Manager* magazine as a top firm in the country for six consecutive years, consistently named in "Who's Who in the World" and "Who's Who in Finance and Industry" by Marquis Publications, listed in *Worth* magazine's Wealth Management Source Book of National Outstanding Advisors, and saluted by both the Palos Verdes and Torrance, Calif. Chambers of Commerce as a top professional firm for more than 10 years.

Stephanie Enright is a financial columnist for the Hearst Corporation's *Daily Breeze* newspaper, the author of several financial books, a member of Vistage, the world's largest presidents' organization, the Women Presidents' Organization, and the International Association of Advisors in Philanthropy.

ADDITIONAL RESOURCES

Chapter 1. Clarity in Financial Goal Planning

- *Personal Finance: Planning and Implementing Your Financial Goals — Desk top Edition* (Wiley, 2007)

- *Personal Finance: Planning and Implementing Your Financial Goals* by Vickie L. Bajtelsmit (Wiley, 2005)

Chapter 2. Investing 101: The Myths, the Facts and All that Lies Between

- *Everybody's Money Book* by Jordan Goodman (Dearborn, 3rd Edition 2001)*

- *The Savage Truth on Money* by Terry Savage (Wiley, 1999)

Chapter 3. Risk: It's a Personal Thing

- *Investment Risk Management* (The Wiley Finance Series) by Yen Yee Chong (Wiley, 2004)

Chapter 4. Protecting Your Assets and Lifestyle from Catastrophic Medical Expenses

- *Health Insurance Resource Manual: Options for People with a Chronic Disease or Disability* by Dorothy E. Northrop and Stephen E. Cooper (Demos Medical Publishing Inc, 2003)

- *Insurance for Dummies* by Jack Hungelmann (Wiley, 2001)

Chapter 5. Retirement Planning

- *Everybody's Money Book on Retirement Planning* by Jordan Goodman (Dearborn, 2002)*

- *Happily Ever After: Expert Advice for Achieving the Retirement of Your Dreams* by Lyn Fisher and Sydney LeBlanc (Financial Forum Publishing, 2007)*

- *The New Retirementality* by Mitch Anthony (Kaplan, 2nd Edition 2006)*

- *Live Long & Prosper! Invest in Your Happiness, Health and Wealth for Retirement and Beyond* by Steve Vernon (Wiley, 2005)*

- *Parlay Your IRA Into a Family Forune* by Ed Slott (Penguin, 2005)*

Chapter 6. Optimizing Your Wealth: Its Not Just About the Money

- *The Number: A Completely Different Way to Think About the Rest of Your Life* by Lee Eisenberg (Free Press, 2006)*

- *Man's Search for Meaning* by Victor Frankl (Washington Square Press, 1985)

Chapter 7. Charitable Giving

- *Halftime: Changing Your Game Plan from Success to Significance* by Bob Buford (Zondervan Publishing House, 1994)

- *Finishing Well: What People Who Really Live Do Differently!* by Bob Buford (Integrity Publishers, 2004)

- *Giving Wisely: Maximizing Your Charitable Giving* by Russ Alan Prince, Chris Blunt & Gary Rathbun (Oscar Printing Company, 2002)*

Chapter 8. Legacy Planning

- *The Survivor Assistance Handbook: A Guide for Financial Transition* by Mark R. Colgan (Mark Colgan, 2007)*

- *Personal Legacy Journal* by Mark Colgan (Mark Colgan, 2006)*

- *The Perfect Legacy: How to Establish Your Own Private Foundation* by Russ Alan Prince, Gary L Rathbun & Karen Maru File (HNW Press, 1998)*

- *Preparing Heirs* by Roy Williams and Vic Preisser (Robert D. Reed Publishers, 2003)

Chapter 9. Wealth Management and the Private Business Owner

- *How to Run Your Business So You Can Leave it in Style* by John H. Brown (Business Enterprise Institute, 1997)

- *Beyond 401(k)s for Small Business Owners: A Practical Guide to Incentive, Deferred Compensation, and Retirement Plans* by Jean D. Sifleet (Wiley 2004)

- *Finance for Non-Financial Managers: And Small Business Owners* by Lawrence W. Tuller (Adams Media Corporation, 1997)

Chapter 10. Definition of a Trusted Advisory Firm

- *The Savvy investor's Guide to Selecting and Evaluating the "Right" Financial Advisor* by Steven R. Drozdeck (Financial Forum Publishing, 2007)*

- *Sins of Ommission: Things Your Broker Should be Telling You* by Michael Kastelnak (Financial Forum Publishing, 3rd Edition 2007)*

---

* This book can be purchased at Financial Forum BOOKstore (http://www.ffbookstore.com) or by calling 435.750.0062.

INDEX